CRITICAL P.
FOR SOCIAL JUSTICE

Critical Pedagogy Today Series

Critical Pedagogy Today provides a range of incisive overviews and applications of Critical Pedagogy across fields and disciplines. Building on the work of Paulo Freire, the series reinvigorates his legacy and provides educators with an array of tools for questioning contemporary practices and forging new pedagogical methods.

Series editors

Shirley R. Steinberg is the Director and Project Leader of the Paulo and Nita Freire International Project for Critical Pedagogy at McGill University.

Ana Maria "Nita" Araujo Freire was Paulo Freire's partner. She taught History of Education in Brazil in colleges and universities in the city of Sao Paulo for many years.

Titles in the Series

On Critical Pedagogy
Henry A. Giroux
2011

Forthcoming:

Rethinking Citizenship: A Theory and Practice of Contemporary Critical Education
Kevin D. Vinson & E. Wayne Ross
2012

Pedagogy of Beauty
Antonia Darder
2012

Critical Pedagogy and Marxism
Peter McLaren
2012

Echoes from Freire for a Critically Engaged Pedagogy
Peter Mayo
2013

Narrative, Learning and Critical Pedagogy
Scherto Gill & Ivor Goodson
2013

CRITICAL PEDAGOGY FOR SOCIAL JUSTICE

JOHN SMYTH

A Series in Celebration of Paula Freire and Joe L. Kincheloe

continuum

2011

Continuum International Publishing Group
80 Maiden Lane, Suite 704, New York, NY 10038
The Tower Building, 11 York Road, London SE1 7NX

www.continuumbooks.com

© John Smyth 2011

Library of Congress Cataloging-in-Publication Data
A catalog record for this book is available from the Library of Congress.

ISBN: 978-1-4411-7669-1 (hardcover)
       978-1-4411-7226-6 (paperback)

Typeset by Newgen Imaging Systems Pvt Ltd, Chennai, India
Printed and bound in the United States of America

Contents

Acknowledgements

Writing is never, for me at least, a process of working totally in isolation or with a 'clean slate', and this book is particularly illustrative of that. Many of the ideas have come out of extensive conversations with my close colleagues Peter McInerney, Barry Down, Lawrence Angus and Tim Harrison, and in an earlier piece, Lyn Fasoli. Joe Kincheloe and Shirley Steinberg, as always, were around my very first piece with Peter Lang Publishing, as was Chris Myers. I am deeply indebted to all of them.

The University of Ballarat, while one of the smallest universities in Australia, has been enormously supportive in providing me with the space to bring this work into existence – and in this I especially salute my supportive, long-time colleague, and Head of School, Lawrence Angus.

Chapter 2: Parts of the this were first published by me as *Critical Politics of Teachers' Work: An Australian Perspective*, pp. 197–206, 2001, reproduced courtesy of Peter Lang Publishing, New York; and 'Critical teaching as the counter-hegemony to neo-liberalism', in S. Macrine, P. McLaren and D. Hill (eds), *Revolutionizing Pedagogy*, pp. 187–209, 2010, reproduced courtesy of Palgrave Macmillan.

Chapter 3: Parts of this were first published by me as 'When students have power', *International Journal of Leadership in Education*, 9(4), 2006, pp. 285–98, reproduced courtesy of Routledge, Taylor and Francis; and 'Climbing over the rocks in the road: the case of

Mango High School' (with Fasoli), Educational Research, **49**(3), 2007, pp. 273–95, reproduced courtesy of Routledge, Taylor and Francis.

Chapter 4: Parts of this were first published by me as 'Schools and communities put at a disadvantage: relational power, resistance, boundary work and capacity building in educational identity formation, *Journal of Learning Communities: International Journal of Learning in Social Contexts*, **3**, 2006, pp. 14–19, reproduced with acknowledgement to Charles Darwin University; and 'Critically engaged community capacity building and the *community organizing* approach to disadvantaged schools', *Critical Studies in Education*, **50**(1), 2009, pp. 10–19, reproduced courtesy of Routledge, Taylor and Francis. Parts of the professional development module *What to look for in **Genuine** Community Engagement – a Toolkit*, (with acknowledgments to my co-authors McInerney and Harrison) are also drawn upon here with grateful acknowledgement to the Victorian Department of Education and Early Childhood Services, the Department of Human Services, and members of the Wendouree West community.

I am also extremely grateful to the Australian Research Council, who have consistently and generously funded my research since 1992 and for the entire period covered by the essays in this book.

No one deserves more commendation for creating the circumstances in which this book was possible than Solvegia – she has been a part of the entire journey, working cheerfully and providing incredible support to this and all my work. I express my love and affection to her for everything!

List of Figures

CHAPTER 1

Critical Hope That Aims to Counter 'the Crippling Fatalism of Neoliberalism'

OPENING EXPLANATORY COMMENT

We need critical hope the way a fish needs unpolluted water.
—Freire, 1996, Pedagogy of Hope

I have chosen to preface this collection of largely reworked essays and papers of mine by trying to get to the essence of Paulo Freire's incredible lifetime project of critical pedagogy, but to do this in a way that brings my own somewhat realistic, while at the same time critical, inflection to it. In doing this, I am deeply indebted to Darren Webb (2010) for his most insightful account, that inspired me to pursue Paulo's quest around the 'need for a kind of educated hope'.

The intent in my opening comments in this overarching piece is to dip into, but only slightly, some of what Webb (2010) has drawn attention to around what Paulo Freire, in A *Pedagogy of Freedom*, termed 'critical hope' (Freire, 1998, p. 70). Before I go into more detail on this crucial idea, I should say something about my wider reason for doing this. My purpose is to provide some kind of intellectual and philosophical scaffolding with which to gain a wider understanding of, while also advancing, a bundle of ideas I have been worrying and interrogating for quite some time.

In accepting Shirley Steinberg and Anna Maria Freire's invitation to contribute to such an important series, I am extremely mindful of wanting to present some ideas that fit with their desire, as series editors, to bring together works that reinvent and improve critical pedagogy for the contemporary – albeit extremely dangerous – times in which we live.

It seemed that my work unquestionably fit their agenda of a pedagogy for social justice, and in what follows I want to unpick the ways in which I pose a discourse of critique around some existing educational and social practices while at the same time providing some pointers to what some more socially just alternatives might look like. I hope that in doing this (and feeling most humbled in the process of even attempting to follow someone with the stature of Freire), I can do justice to the spirit of Paulo's notion of radical education as a project that is always incomplete and in the process of transformation.

I could have taken off in a multitude of different directions in this book – indeed, my commissioning prospectus suggested an extraordinarily ambitious, but ultimately unachievable, constellation of topics. Instead, I have deliberately reigned myself in, in order to meet the editorial requirement of a shorter document that might be accessible to diverse audiences, possibly from cross-disciplinary backgrounds, while able to be accessed through a semester-long window, possibly as a supplementary course text. Hence my quite deliberate triumvirate of the following:

- teachers – as intellectuals;
- students – as activists;
- communities – as politically engaged and connected.

I think this nested troika provides me with an ideal way in which to explore what a critical praxis within and between these topics might look like.

EDUCATED HOPE – A PROLEGOMENON

I am not equipped by training or disposition to explore the philosophical and theological complexities of reading of Freire's notion of critical hope in the way Webb (2010) has already done. Nor is that appropriate or necessary in this introductory essay. Rather, my intent here is to provide a brief glimpse into a crucial and fascinating aspect of Freire's works and then to leave the reader to pursue them in depth elsewhere, while I deploy some of these ideas in subsequent chapters to make a bridge to my own work. Many of Freire's comments in this regard were made up to four decades ago, and they are as challenging, potent and relevant today as when they were initially made.

For starters, Freire's central notion is that 'hope', as an idea, 'is rooted in [our] incompleteness', and that *what makes us human* is the 'constant search' to become more fulfilled. This is something we pursue collaboratively and in communion with others – a theme that was given particular expression in his defining *Pedagogy of the Oppressed* (1972a, p. 64, my emphasis). This notion is considerably at variance with the dominance of neoliberal ideas today, in which the overwhelming emphasis is upon individualism, materialism, consumption and personal acquisition.

The latter are ideas that Ira Shor pursued in conversation with Paulo Freire in A *Pedagogy for Liberation: Dialogues on Transforming Education* (Shor and Freire, 1987). Ira summed it up in respect to US society (although as a non-American, I would argue it applies equally to all other western societies) as follows:

> With our deep roots in individualism . . . [we have a] devotion to 'making it on your own', improving yourself, moving up in the world, pulling yourself up by your own bootstraps, striking it rich by an ingenious personal effort. (p. 110)

Shor goes on to point out that this misplaced emphasis on individualism is a chimera – an evaporating myth:

> This emphasis on 'self' is the educational equivalent of the capitalist infatuation with the lone entrepreneur, that romantic and fading factor in an economy now monopolized by giant corporations. (p. 110)

'Hopelessness', according to Freire (1972a, p. 64) is 'a form of silence' that amounts to a gross case of denial of the world. It is akin to 'fleeing from it' (p. 64). To be fully human, he says, is tantamount to confronting the world, challenging it, asking questions about how the social relations we live by have been constructed and what it is that keeps these relations in place. To put this even more sharply, Freire (1972a) argues that 'hope . . . does not consist of folding one's arms and waiting' (p. 64). For him, this kind of passivism is 'empty and sterile' and is likely to invoke from us encounters and responses that are 'bureaucratic and tedious' (p. 64). To embrace the world in static or inert ways is to be infused with fear – the very antithesis of risk – which underpins critical approaches to thinking and learning.

From this vantage point, we can begin to envisage all kinds of possibilities. For example, notions of 'not learning' or 'failure' to become engaged with school learning – which frequently ends up being falsely labeled as 'dropping out' of school – could be considered as an illustration of a failure to teach what is meant by hope. Invoking the work of Snyder (2002), Webb (2010) says that people who are labeled 'hopeless' (p. 328) are quite literally that way 'because they were not taught to think in this manner' (Snyder, 2002, p. 253). This is a very different inflection to the notion of 'failure', which in common parlance is taken to mean failure to achieve or learn due to a lack of application, aptitude or effort. This positions failure, and who and what has failed, in a very different light.

4

Webb (2010) goes to some considerable lengths to draw our attention to Freire's mindfulness of false, simplistic, unsophisticated, undisciplined and naïve approaches to hope – which can only end up in 'frustration', 'disappointment', 'despair' and 'immobilization' (p. 334). As Freire (1996) states in *Pedagogy of Hope*: 'hope, as an ontological need, demands an anchoring in practice' (p. 9) – something that I will demonstrate in later chapters as a feature of my own attempt to follow Freire's project of cultural action.

Freire (1996) argues that in developing this focused approach we need passion, commitment and persistence, but equally 'we must take every care not to experience [hope] in a mistaken form' – by which he means approaches that are 'vain', 'frivolous', 'reckless', 'irresponsible', 'over-zealous' and that lose their 'grip on reality' (Webb, 2010, p. 334). In other words, hope needs to be tempered by a high level of realism. Developing this kind of disposition, Freire (1996) says, requires 'serious . . . political analysis' to enable us 'to unveil opportunities . . . no matter what the obstacles may be' (p. 9). Grace (1994) labels this 'complex hope', which means 'recogniz[ing] the historical and structural difficulties which have to be overcome' (p. 57). This seems to me to be simply prudent! In *Daring to Dream: Toward a Pedagogy of the Unfinished*, Freire (2007) urges us to 'speak about . . . limits' (p. 64) and to discuss what can be accomplished 'where', 'how', 'with whom' and 'when' (p. 64), and in the process to realize that our work as educators 'is not individual, but social, and that it takes place within the social practice he or she is a part of' (pp. 64–5). Carlson (2005) captures this point in his study of democratic renewal in a high school when he says we need to 'construct narratives of hope without illusion' and that doing so involves a recognition 'that culture is contested and thus open rather than determined' (p. 21).

Part of Freire's argument in *Cultural Action for Freedom* (Freire, 1972b) is that the forces of domination 'have nothing to announce but the preservation of the *status quo*', with the result that they are totally committed to the 'domestication of the future' (Webb, 2010, p. 331) in order to ensure that it is a tame 'repetition of the present' (Freire, 1972b, p. 41). In *Daring to Dream*, Freire (2007) responds to this construction of inequality and deprivation by labelling them a 'resounding obscenity' (p. 22). What we see coming through here is the notion that critical hope is not about being 'patient and serene' (Webb, 2010, p. 334); rather it is infused with 'outrage, indignation and restlessness' (p. 333). Neither is there unrealism about timelines or what can be achieved within them, but rather a process of calculative 'active waiting' (p. 333), nicely captured in the title of Freire's (2004) book, *Pedagogy of Indignation*. Freire (1972a) put it in these terms in *Pedagogy of the Oppressed*: 'As long as I fight I am moved by hope: and if I fight with hope then I can wait' (p. 64).

GETTING 'CONTROL OF DESTINY'

Duncan-Andrade (2009) is especially helpful in the way he confronts and challenges a range of what he calls 'enemies of hope' and the effects these have on groups placed at the bottom of the social gradient. He labels these variants of false hope 'hokey hope', 'mythical hope' and 'hope deferred', and his argument is that these constitute a collective, illusory framework that in the end presents an entirely misleading facsimile of the real thing.

'Hokey hope' (which is derived from 'hokum', meaning, bunkum, sensational, sentimental or unreal), is based, as Duncan-Andrade (2009) puts it, on the naïve view that somehow things will get better, even when there is no evidence to warrant this view and even less indication as to how the existing situation might be changed. Hokey hope is false and misleading because it flies in the face of and 'ignores the laundry list of inequalities that impact the lives [of excluded groups]' (p. 182), and it denies the demonstrably uneven playing field upon which their lives are lived and experienced. The consequence of this unreality is that relationships get played out in veneered, synthetic and entirely 'pragmatic' ways. For example, in the educational arena, we see relationships dominated through 'impersonal and objective language, including such terms as goals, strategies, and standardized curriculum' that are unashamedly used to justify 'decisions made by one group for another' (Valenzuela, 1999, p. 22).

Duncan-Andrade (2009) puts his criticism in the most direct and sharp way when he points to hokey hope as amounting to a form of 'false caring . . . in which the more powerful members of a relationship define themselves as caring despite the fact that the recipients of the so-called caring do not perceive it as such' (p. 183). Hokey hope is thus predicated on a 'middle-class opportunity structure that is inaccessible to the overwhelming majority' (p. 183) of the social groups it is supposed to benefit. Even more problematic is the way in which it 'largely delegitimizes the pain [experienced by such groups] as a result of a persistently unequal society' and positions them such that the privileged and oblivious class, who persistently fail to understand the plight of the less advantaged, are prepared to metaphorically 'let them eat cake' (p. 183).

'Mythical hope', on the other hand, has some of the same features, with the addition of a 'false narrative of equality of opportunity', which is completely evacuated of any sense of the history or politics of how inequality has been created and is sustained. There is a kind of mythmaking taking place here, asserting that somehow people who have been *placed at a disadvantage* (my terminology and emphasis) can transcend the obstacles and succeed despite adversity. The most disturbing aspect of mythical hope, as Duncan-Andrade (2009) states, is its 'profoundly ahistorical and depoliticized denial of suffering that is rooted in celebrating individual exceptions' (p. 184). In other words, in accordance with mythical hope, anyone can succeed, despite debilitating backgrounds, provided they make the appropriate investment of effort; and there are many examples that can be cited of people who have done this – albeit, the pathways they have taken to overcome obstacles in a way that has fundamentally transformed the land-scapes from which they have come remain unclear. These are serendipitous instances that come across more as lone examples of successful escapees than they do as stories of transformations of the underlying conditions that remain uninterrupted and as a result continue to afflict others.

'Hope deferred', Duncan-Andrade's (2009) third variant, involves shifting the focus, albeit only a little, by avoiding out-right 'blaming the victim' and instead pointing the finger of blame at 'the economy', 'the lack of social services' or 'the system' (p. 184) – all of which largely miss the mark, because their super-ficiality masks their inability to manifest 'any kind of transforma-tive pedagogical project' (p. 184). Underlying deferred hope is the vain wish that somehow society will undergo some kind of reform that will enable those excluded to magically ascend to the middle class. This kind of hope is manifestly unreal, because as Duncan-Andrade (2009), invoking Syme (2004), argues, it fails to under-stand the powerful effect of the absence of 'control of destiny' (p. 184). By this term Syme (2004) means 'the ability of people to deal with the forces that affect their lives (even if they decide not to deal with them)' (p. 3).

The argument being rehearsed here by Syme (2004) around 'control of destiny' and reinforced by epidemiological research (Wilkinson and Marmot, 2003; Wilkinson, 2005; Marmot, 2007; 2010; Wilkinson and Pickett, 2009) is that social groups who experience 'chronic stress' on a prolonged basis are susceptible to becoming sick because inequalities expose them such that 'their primary human needs [are] under constant attack' (Duncan-Andrade, 2009, p. 185). Refusal to confront and address these realities of social inequality and, in the process, to 'cultivate their control of destiny' (p. 185) in the social groups concerned, means that all we have left to offer them is 'hope deferred' (p. 185). That is to say, what they need to do is get better at setting individual goals and targets for themselves and they will make it. The problem with this line is that wearing the problem individually in this way belies the fact that those who are supposed to be working with and for such groups are themselves unprepared to make 'the level of sacrifices' (p. 185) necessary to close the gap, and the result is sadly predictable.

What 'control of destiny' means, practically speaking, is being prepared to reframe the issues in other ways – ways that are more mindful of the real lives and circumstances of the people most directly affected. To take an example from another area, as Syme (2004) argued in his work regarding the attempt to reduce the health effects of smoking, focusing on disease and risk factors is unlikely to work when people have other, more pressing priorities in their lives. Coming at the issue by getting people to articulate how reducing smoking or substance use might affect hopes they have for the future might have possibilities. For example, working with them on

> ways of implementing their dreams; how to make things work for their benefit; how to select a problem and succeed in solving it; how to develop strategies for getting done what they want to get done; how to take control of their destiny. (p. 3)

CRITICAL HOPE – THE REAL DEAL!

This brings us to the alternative to these various versions of 'false hope'. Duncan-Andrade (2009) identifies three aspects – what he calls 'material hope', which acknowledges the existence of spaces, cracks and crevices within which resistance can and does occur; 'Socratic hope', which involves developing the courage and the solidarity with which to pursue alternatives in dialogue with others; and 'audacious hope', which equips young people and their communities with the courage and the strategies to 'speak back' to inequities.

9

'Audacious hope' has two parts to it. First, an acknowledgement that positions and stances have to be adopted collectively, by schools, parents, communities and other groups working together, and that little can be achieved by working separately; and second, audacious hope goes beyond individual responses by being daring, somewhat bold and intrepid in insisting that things be questioned in deeper ways – ways that question, challenge and confront the source of how things are made the way they are and how some people continue to benefit, often in obscene ways, through advantage or privilege.

At this point, Duncan-Andrade (2009) provides a useful illustration of what this means. To regard educational success as residing entirely at the level of individual effort is to deny the collective pain and suffering of those who don't have the cultural and social attributes with which to succeed. He provides as an example the way in which schools deal with student emotions: schools expect young people to metaphorically park their emotions at the school gate at the beginning of each day. As any teacher or researcher who has spent time in non-middle-class schools will attest, the reality is that emotions in these contexts regularly overflow into classrooms. The conventional response is that emotional and what are labelled 'behavioural' infractions are handled in schools by invoking behaviour-management policies. Duncan-Andrade (2009) says that schools and individual teachers respond in this way so as to maintain classrooms as 'spaces that are safe from righteous rage' (p. 190). The corollary to this is that policies and plans that are designed to manage and 'weed out' children who display inappropriate behaviour occur at the expense of exploring better ways of helping students to channel their responses. He uses an ecological analogy, likening the interdependency of what occurs to a 'micro-ecosystem' of the classroom. What goes on in the classroom today has long and complex tentacles that reach into the open social systems that students inhabit, and trying to deal with behaviour issues in a hermetically sealed way is an exercise doomed to certain failure. Students in schools are not sealed off from the 'external [social] toxins' when they come into schools and classrooms, and these toxins have a powerful effect on their willingness to learn.

Duncan-Andrade's (2009) point is that while he might not be personally able to control the passage of these toxins into his classroom, he can control how he responds to them in his classroom. He says 'This gives me, and my students, the audacity to hope' (p. 190)—for a different way of reacting, responding and analysing. His wider point is that expelling a 'disobedient' and unruly child from the classroom might seem to have removed a behavioural problem, but this might be at the very considerable expense of creating an even worse problem by corroding 'trust', diminishing 'hope' and conveying messages about lack of 'care', all of which are crucial bases to learning. 'Weeding out' trouble-makers in order to allow others to learn uninterrupted might seem logical and rational at one level, but doing so strikes at the heart of the preconditions of self-esteem, trust and care that are the pillars of learning outcomes.

Impetuous, short-term responses 'seriously underestimate the impact our response has on the other students in the class' (p. 191), who see the short-term trade-off of the need for orderliness as being against the long-term relational goodwill that is the bedrock of their collective learning. Other students are powerful witnesses of this loss of relational trust and can only be left wondering where it leaves them should they find themselves in the same place as their unfortunate peers.

This line of argument was well captured by the assistant principal I interviewed and report on in Chapter 3, who said of the young people in his 'disadvantaged' high school: 'these kids learn the teachers first, then the subjects' (Chapter 3, p. 88). This is clearly a take on Kohl's (1994) notion 'I won't learn from you', summarized by Duncan-Andrade's (2009) 'students try not to learn from teachers who don't authentically care about them', for the self-evident reason that 'students don't care what you know until they know you care' (p. 191).

This is a theme I explore in more detail in Chapter 3 through an actual case study of a school I call Mango High School. Suffice, for the moment, to say that how we as educators respond to 'willed not learning' (Kohl, 1994, p. 27) has much to do with how willing we are to challenge educational issues that allegedly require conventional 'solutions' with more audacious and cheeky responses. This is where the licensing of audacious hope comes in, together with courage and solidarity, and on this it is worth finishing this introductory chapter with a comment from Kohl (1994):

> Willed not learning consists of a conscious and chosen refusal to assent to learn. It manifests itself most often in withdrawal or defiance and is not just a school-related phenomenon (p. 27) . . . Since students have no way to legitimately criticize the schooling they are subjected to or the people they are required to learn from, resistance and rebellion are stigmatized. The system's problem becomes the victim's problem. However, willed not-learning is a healthy, though frequently dysfunctional, response to racism, sexism, and other forms of bias.' (p. 29)

CHAPTER 2

Teachers-as-Intellectuals in Neoliberal Times

PREAMBLE

In this chapter, I want to revisit and explore an issue I first canvassed in my writing as far back as 1987, in the context of Henry Giroux's writing on the topic of teachers-as-intellectuals and his seminal book the following year (Giroux, 1988), *Teachers as Intellectuals: Toward a Critical Pedagogy of Learning*. It seems that the more times change, the more things stay the same (or even worsen) at a fundamental level. At the heart of the issue is the nature of the work of teaching, and following on from that, some thorny and enduring questions – what is teaching, who has an opinion about it, who has the right to conceptualize it and, in the end, who controls it?

I need to briefly revisit some urgent issues I examined some time ago in order to bring into sharper focus the implications they hold for socially just approaches to schooling in contemporary times.

This chapter has two major parts to it: (1) an argument about the inherently intellectual nature of teachers' work and the way it is being compromised, corrupted and corroded by 'management pedagogies' – and of the need to robustly confront these; and (2) a portrayal of what a 'critical re-imagining of teaching' might look like that rehabilitates the intellectual and political in teaching and that advocates for social responsibility and social justice. The chapter concludes with an indication of what such a critical imaginary of teaching looks like at the level of the classroom and it makes the case for the pressing urgency to do so in the dangerous times we live in.

THE BASIS OF THE ARGUMENT

Generally speaking, teachers can hardly be regarded as an 'oppressed' group in the way we conventionally understand and deploy that term. They are generally well off and well-paid, and have significant social status – that is, until we look a little closer and deeper.

It is not hard to make a compelling case that as a large occupational group, teachers around the world have been universally and systematically dealt with harshly by neo-liberal reform policies for more than three decades. In particular, regardless of where we look, teachers have been systematically excluded from and denied a voice in the nature of reforms to the work of teaching. Their views have been denigrated, effaced, expunged and laminated over in terms of having any legitimacy.

Furthermore, their work has been shamefully exploited in ways that are allegedly in the interests of the economy (under the argument of international economic competitiveness) – which is really a thinly veiled code for transnational economic colonialism and subjugation. It would not be an exaggeration to claim that the work of teachers has largely been rendered down to that of being mere 'technicians' – implementing the technical/instrumental 'how to' agenda, while all the important educational questions are decided by others far removed from schools, classrooms and communities. This exclusion from being able to ask 'what and why' questions amounts to a process of 'deskilling' teachers, as control over their work is increasingly diverted to impersonal mechanisms of surveillance.

One of the most salient consequences of this 'technical turn' is that teachers have been forced to become complicit in the perpetration of a myth – that of 'skills formation', within a narrow and diminished version of vocationalism – when the reality is that the jobs of future workers (i.e. current students) are being relentlessly exported overseas to places with lower labour costs.

Another expression of this impotence is the way teachers have become implicated in the requirement to convert schools into citadels of 'consumption' – under snake-oil rubrics like 'self-management', 'devolution' and 'school choice' – in which parents are left no choice other than to 'shop around' for the best individual deal for their children. The effect has been to leach out or downgrade the notion of any collective benefit accruing to education, while at the same time moving apace with the privatization of public schools via the back door, thus effectively dismantling publicly provided education in all but name.

The insertion of proxy parental consumption devices, such as 'choice', into schools to ensure that teachers do their 'economic work' (Smyth and Shacklock, 1998, chapter 4) has brought with it a range of disfiguring devices which have been let loose on schools, such as high stakes testing regimes, league tables and marketized approaches of image and impression management.

The obliteration and obfuscation of the vernacular language and discourse of teaching and teachers' work, and its replacement with synthetic, alien, interloping and improper managerialist (and spurious economistic) discourses, has brought with it toxic practices now familiar to every classroom teacher, such as outcomes, benchmarking, standards, competencies, accountability, performance management, performance (payments by results) pay, value added, and world's 'best practice' – to mention only a few.

Increasing central control over teaching has been further aided and abetted through the perpetration of the process of 'steering' at a distance that brings with it the by now familiar forms of centralized curriculum frameworks and guidelines, delivery targets and performance indicators – all of which have led to the further cumulative immiseration, demoralization and marginalization of teaching as a valued occupation.

Against this ideological and technicized onslaught, what is the alternative?

TEACHING AS INTELLECTUAL WORK

To reconceptualize teachers' work as a form of intellectual labour amounts to encouraging teachers to critically question their understandings of society, schooling and pedagogy. It involves acknowledging the claim made by Kohl (1983) about the need for teachers to be actively responsible for theory making (and theory testing) or accept the fact that these will be made for teachers by academic researchers and others only too willing to assume that task.

What is important here is not the emphasis on the intellectual per se, but rather the political, social and moral imperatives of uncontested power, authority and domination which such a perspective opens up for critique and action. In proposing a focus on 'the intellectual', it is not being suggested that teachers become aloof, abstract or detached from the real world of teaching – this is a misconstrual of what it means to be an intellectual. Gramsci (1971) argues that what is important about intellectual work, and hence the activities of intellectuals, is not their cognitive function, often seen as existing independently of issues of class, culture and power, but rather their political and social prowess in developing the potential to engage with and transform dominant theoretical traditions. Kohl (1983) claims that an intellectual is a person who 'knows about his or her field, has a wide breadth of knowledge about other aspects of the world, who uses experience to develop theory, and questions theory on the basis of further experience' (p. 30). But, even more important than that, Kohl (1983) argues that an intellectual is above all 'someone who has the courage to question authority and who refuses to act counter to his/her own experience and judgment' (p. 30). Greene (1985) claims that many teachers fail to do so

> because the processes that go on in their institutions strike them as so automatic, there seems to be no alternative but to comply. Their schools seem to resemble natural processes; what happens in them appears to have the sanction of natural law and can no more be questioned or resisted than the law of gravity. (p. 11)

It was Gramsci (1971) who argued the more general case for reclaiming the theoretical tradition of the intellectual, and Aronowitz and Giroux (1985) and Giroux (1985a,b,c) who gave expression and impetus to those ideas in the context of education and schooling. Their work is closely associated with Gramsci's (1971) challenge to the allegedly value-free neutral nature of intellectual activity; it is this that represents his major theoretical advance. His disavowal of the intellectual as being apolitical is well put by Giroux (1985b) when he says,

> Inherent in such a view is the notion that the intellectual is obligated to engage in a value free discourse, one that necessitates that he or she refuses to take sides on different issues, or refuses to link knowledge with fundamental principles of emancipation. Such a view reinforces the idea that intellectuals are free floating and detached in the sense that they perform a type of labor that is objective and apolitical. (p. 86)

The essence of Giroux and McLaren's (1986) argument is that a reconstitution of teachers' work will result in teachers being construed as

> bearers of critical knowledge, rules and values through which they consciously articulate and problematize their relationship

to each other, to students, to subject matter, and to the wider community. This view of authority exposes and challenges the dominant view of teachers as primarily technicians or public servants whose role is to implement rather than to conceptualize pedagogical practice. Moreover, the category of emancipatory authority dignifies teacher work by viewing it as an intellectual practice with respect to both its formal characteristics and the nature of the content discussed. Teachers' work becomes a form of intellectual labor opposed to the pedagogical divisions between conception and practice, and production and implementation, that are currently celebrated in a number of educational reforms. The concept of teacher as intellectual carries with it the political and ethical imperative to judge, critique, and reject those approaches to authority that reinforce a technical and social division of labor that silences and disempowers both teachers and students. (pp. 225–6)

What is significant about this reconceptualization of teachers' work is that it provides a basis from which to argue against the encroachment of those bent on treating teaching as a particular species of instrumentalism. This should not be interpreted as a narrow claim to change the teaching role. On the contrary, what is being argued for is a change in perspective by those outside of schools, away from a particular limited view of pedagogy. While it is true that pedagogy refers to a general systematic procedure for advancing learning, there is also a sense in which to act pedagogically means to act in ways that 'empower' learners. Pedagogues ask questions while articulating their theories about teaching and learning – they verbalize why they do what they do in their teaching, interrogating their knowing so as to uncover why it is that they accept current practices and questioning the veracity of the social conditions that support and sustain them. In Simon (1985) and Giroux's (1985a) terms, this amounts to a 'critical pedagogy' in which knowing is an ideological process

18

that requires continual clarification and elaboration of the relationship between knowledge and the social order. According to Simon (1985), the various ways of knowing are in fact organized around particular 'taken-for-granted' assumptions and practices that permit certain questions to be posed, while actively suppressing others.

What is needed is a way of reclaiming knowledge about teaching that acknowledges and questions its socially construed nature and the way it relates to the social order. The following questions represent some examples:

- Why do I insist on external rewards and punishments to make kids learn?
- Why do I define the 'good' kids as the 'quiet' kids?
- Why is it that I insist on equating 'workbook work' with 'reading'?
- Why do I regard 'on-task time' as synonymous with 'learning'?
- Why is it that I have come to regard 'getting through the material' as the prime goal of my teaching?

Questioning habitual pedagogical practices in this way necessitates asking other pointed questions that seek to unravel the social, cultural and political forces that have shaped our teaching and that actually prevent us from dislodging those deeply entrenched practices embedded in questions such as the following:

- Where do my ideas about teaching/learning come from historically?
- How did I come to appropriate these ideas, anyway?
- What social and cultural conditions cause me to continue to endorse the ideas I hold to be true about teaching/learning?
- Whose interests do my ideas actually serve?
- What power relationships between myself and my students are expressed in my teaching practices?

- Do my practices accommodate to the dominant ideology?
- How do I encourage resistance by those who are oppressed?
- In view of this, are there grounds for radically changing the way I teach?

To regard teaching in this way is to adopt a viewpoint that involves critique and transformation. Simon (1985) argues that such a 'transformative critique' has three interrelated moments:

> First, transformative critique views knowledge as socially pro- duced, legitimated, and distributed and seeks to make explicit the ways in which such production, legitimation, and dis- tribution take place. Second, knowledge is apprehended as expressing and embodying particular interests and values, implicating issues of power and ethics in all expressions of knowledge. Third, seeking to negate the 'objective' nature of knowledge and forcing the educator to confront the relation between knowledge, power, and control, critique additionally requires the articulation and consideration of transformative action – that is, action that would alter the distribution of power and increase the range and scope of possibilities for individually and collectively defined projects. (p. 1119)

Giroux and McLaren (1986) argue that what is involved here is a process in which teaching and learning are 'linked to the more political goal of educating students to take risks and to struggle with on-going relations of power in order to alter the oppressive conditions in which life is lived' (p. 226). All of this recognizes that schools are socially constructed realities in which there are continuous struggles among contending groups to have their par- ticular lived reality of schooling recognized.

Adopting a critical stance towards teaching and learning, there- fore, involves more than being negative and carping (Carr and Kemmis, 1983). It requires, as Apple (1975) claims, a painful process of radically examining our current positions and asking pointed questions about the relationship that exists between these positions and the social structure from which they arise. It also necessitates a serious in-depth search for alternatives to these almost unconscious lenses we employ and an ability to cope with an ambiguous situation for which answers can now be only dimly seen and which will not be easy to come by. (p. 127)

ARGUING FOR A CRITICAL PEDAGOGY OF TEACHING

A critical pedagogy of schooling, therefore, goes considerably beyond a 'reflective' approach to teaching. For Giroux (1983), the defect of the reflective approach is that it is severely constrained and limited by what it ignores. Being critical, or engaging in critique, involves analysis, enquiry and critique into the transformative possibilities implicit in the social context of classrooms and schooling itself. The intent of critical pedagogy is that of 'liberation' (or emancipation), in the sense that people

are increasingly free to choose from a range of alternative perspectives on themselves and their social worlds. This freedom of choice requires the ability to see one's own views of what is good or right, possible or impossible, true or false, as problematic, socially constructed, and subject to social and political influence. (Berlak, 1985, p. 2)

A truly critical pedagogy involves an examination of existing social relationships at three levels: that of history, of current practice (including its hierarchical bases) and of the potential to transform arrangements in the future. Simon (1984) claims that to act critically means figuring out

why things are the way they are, how they got that way, and what set of conditions are supporting the processes that maintain

21

them. Further . . . we must be able to evaluate the potential for action that [is] embedded in actual relationships. To think these tasks through requires concepts that can carry a critique of existing practice. (p. 380)

Where the critical perspective becomes especially poignant is in situations (such as the current one) in which there are intensified moves towards increased centralism in education, with their reductionist and predetermined curriculum guidelines, frameworks and packages, and concomitant prescription of pedagogical procedures. This trend, which is part of a much broader attempt to deskill workers generally (Braverman, 1975), is at least partly obscured by the allegedly benign technical nature of work and its objectivist claims to be concerned only with managerialist matters of efficiency and effectiveness in schooling. As we know, such approaches are far from being value free; they have a well-developed corporatist agenda designed, among other things, to get teachers to 'lift their game'.

Because of economic crises facing governments and the tightening fiscal squeeze, it has not been difficult for policy makers to generate politically compelling arguments about the need to ensure value for the taxpayer's beleaguered educational dollar. The emphasis has been upon the economic rationalization of educational systems, with the requirement that teachers attend to the business management canons of 'standardization', 'efficiency' and 'effectiveness'. The push for economic accountability in education has meant an intensification of moves towards the scientific management of schools and school systems.

The problem with the technocratic view of education and teaching is that the emphasis on 'excellence', 'quality', 'efficiency' and 'effectiveness' severely brings into question the ability of teachers to provide the kind of intellectual and moral leadership necessary to enable children to be educated. What are rehearsed are liturgical solutions regarding what is considered by some to be important in schooling. What is not opened up for debate and contestation are the fundamental deficiencies in the ways schools are conceived and organized. What we have, therefore, is what Giroux (1979) terms 'a dispending of the culture of positivism' which serves only to bolster and reproduce the orthodox view of what schools and teaching are about.

The discourse of management pedagogy that has muscled its way into schools has brought with it the larger agenda of supplanting the idiosyncratic and value-laden experiences of classrooms, teachers and students. But herein lies the curious paradox – there is also a simultaneous and continuous struggle against the goals and objectives set by others outside of class-rooms. This becomes clearer when we accept a 'dialectical' view of power that amounts to a working against frozen social relationships that constrain and deny transformative possibili-ties. As Giddens (1979) put it,

> Power relations . . . are always two-way, even if the power of one actor or party in a social relation is minimal compared to another. Power relations are relations of autonomy and depen-dence, but even the most autonomous agent is in some degree dependent, and the most dependent actor or party in a relation-ship retains some autonomy. (p. 93)

CHALLENGING 'MANAGEMENT PEDAGOGIES'

If teachers are to challenge and ultimately supplant this domi-nant technocratic view of schooling, then it is necessary that they be articulate about the nature of their work and where they are located historically and pedagogically in it, while also being conscious of its social and political purposes. It means teach-ers must go beyond the roles of technicians, managers or effi-cient clerks imposed upon them by others and be unwilling to continue to accept the way things are in schools. Even when these externally contrived agenda appear to be rational, sensible and humane, the inability of management pedagogies to adequately understand, let alone grapple with, the complexities in classrooms creates a situation of opposition for teachers. What must not be overlooked (cf. Smyth, 1986) is that unequal power relations in schools (between individuals and groups) are *established* and *constructed* through the lived experiences of people in schools. As such, they can be 'disestablished' and 'deconstructed' in the way people choose to live, work and ultimately penetrate the object of their struggles. What is needed is a faith in the power of teachers to reflect upon, resist and change the oppressive circumstances in which they find themselves (Giroux, 1981, p. 216).

As Giroux (1985a) argues, what is at stake is not simply disempowerment of teachers who are losing control of the basic conditions of their work, but rather that the increasing technicist burdens being imposed on teachers to implement the dictates of educational experts is altering the fundamental division of labour and thereby changing teachers' own perceptions of their role as reflective practitioners. To counter this tendency teachers must engage in the creation of a culture of teaching in which the agenda is one of rendering problematic the very cultural forms and content of classroom instruction itself. McLaren (1986) put it in these terms:

> Once we understand the classroom as an embattled symbolic arena where classroom and street discourses collide and where teachers and classroom peer groups struggle over how reality is to be signified, and in what manner and style the cultural terrain is to be engaged, then we, as teachers can begin to situate classroom reform in both the fight for material equality and the forging of a new symbolic sphere. (McLaren, 1986, pp. 253–4)

To regard teachers' work as a form of intellectual labour is to endorse Freire's (1972a) 'problem posing' view of education, in which actors 'develop their power to perceive critically the way they exist in the world with which and in which they find themselves; they come to see the world not as a static reality, but as a reality in process, in transformation' (p. 56).

What this amounts to is a form of 'resistance' – a way for teachers and students to mediate the contradictory lived experiences of schooling so as to address the problems of the hidden curriculum (Apple, 1971). For Giroux (1983) this involves more than mere oppositional behavior which, while it is active, does not address the underlying issues of domination. He argues that resistance involves 'uncovering the degree to which . . . [action] speaks to a form of refusal that highlights . . . the need to struggle against the social nexus of domination and submission' (p. 109). Giroux's (1983) notion of power (which he sees as being inextricably connected to knowledge) is closely tied to his view of resistance. For him, rather than power being unidirectional, he sees it as permitting and encouraging 'progressive alternatives' even within the most hierarchical and oppressive of relationships. By way of example, he says, 'Within most authoritative modes of classroom discipline and control there are fleeting images of freedom that speak to very different relationships' (p. 79). It is in this context that Giroux (1985b) sees teachers as 'resisting intellectuals' capable of inserting education into the political sphere 'by arguing that schooling represents a struggle over power relations' (p. 87). He sees students as also having to be involved in the struggle to overcome injustices and to humanize themselves in the process. Doing this requires giving students not only 'an active voice in their own learning experiences' (p. 87) but also ways of engaging in critique so as to see the relationship between problems of everyday life and the pedagogical practices enacted in classrooms.

This means rejecting the instrumentalist transmission view of education in which external experts determine content which is then relayed to passive students; it requires in its place a radically different alternative (Shor, 1980). It means accepting that knowledge does not exist independently of the meaning and significance which students attach to it by virtue of their previous experiences, their class and their culture. Unlike behaviourist forms of knowledge, this approach to knowledge does not attempt to 'place beyond criticism what is always potentially contentious' (Ryan, 1982, p. 25). Rather, it is concerned with teachers and students working in ways that challenge 'culturally-induced distortions' and allow 'previously-submerged insights' (Ryan, 1982, p. 25) to surface and provide the basis for a variety of pedagogical strategies. Clearly, such reflective and inquiring approaches are at variance with centrally prescribed curriculum guidelines and viewpoints that are concerned with cost-effective systems of educational delivery.

As long as technocrats are allowed to co-opt and domesticate educational thinking and discourse within an outcomes-oriented managerialist ideology, then educational debate will be restricted to a concern about a sterile measuring of results against objectives. The bigger questions about the nature of the 'educational good' will continue to go unanswered. As Van Manen (1977) put it, a preoccupation with technical concerns actively prevents a consideration of the inequitable nature of the society we live in and of the role schools play in maintaining that inequality. The consequence is that teachers are increasingly forced into a situation of 'epistemological consumerism' in which the kind of choices that exist are from the growing array of curriculum, evaluation and pedagogy hawked around by others. For Van Manen (1977) the danger in this instrumentalist 'expert–user' dichotomy lies in its superficial understanding of both the interpretive and critical processes of teaching and learning.

If, as Apple (1983) argues, western societies are becoming increasingly caught up in fiscal crises, then mass produced materials become a de facto mechanism for effectively exercising centralized control over schools and trivializing the nature of teachers' work. There is a deskilling process at work whereby teachers are robbed of their creativity and initiative (Apple and Teitelbaum, 1986), which are replaced by

> a call for the separation of conception from execution; the standardization of school knowledge in the interest of managing and controlling it; and the devaluation of critical, intellectual work on the part of teachers and students for the primacy of practical considerations. (Giroux, 1985c, p. 377)

In this scheme, teachers are seen as passive recipients who act as 'executors' of 'the laws and principles of effective teaching' (Zeichner, 1983, p. 4), and it is this ideology that impregnates documents like the US Department of Education's (1986) *What Works: Research About Teaching and Learning*. While trying to espouse an honest broker role, this document (and others like it) posit normative structures about teaching and learning that standardize pedagogical practice. While making a pretence to objectivity and claims to tentativeness by virtue of only including those research findings 'about which research evidence and expert opinions were consistent, persuasive, and fairly stable over time' (p. 1), the broader political agenda is to establish and maintain a conservative and uncritical view of teaching and learning. Recommendations in the form of recipes for action are put for the alleged benefit of teachers, parents and educational communities on the virtues and values of: increased homework; enhanced time-on task; application and hard work; high teacher expectations; direct instruction and rote learning; frequent testing; subject matter rigour; preparation for the world of work; and the like.

Far from actually emancipating or liberating teachers, corporatist measures such as these serve to further entrench feelings of subservience and dependence among teachers. There is no sense in which action of this kind invests teachers with the capacity to explore, understand and transform their own thinking about the means and the ends of teaching (Smyth, 1984; 1985). Instead, there is a kind of educational consumerism in which the relations are those between 'supplier' – and 'customer – with educational research acting to amass scientific evidence in support of the need for more 'educational packages' and for their more accurate 'delivery to the consumer' (Illich, cited in Fried, 1980, p. 5)

By reconstruing the nature of teachers' work, as is being argued for here, so as to emphasize its intellectual nature, it becomes possible to locate changes in teaching within the broader transformations occurring in the workforce generally. We are able to see, for example, how the devaluation of teachers' work is part of a more general process of the degradation of labour (Braverman, 1975). It becomes clearer, too, that the category of the intellectual is helpful in providing 'a theoretical basis for examining teacher work as a form of intellectual labor, as opposed to defining it purely in instrumental or technical terms' (Giroux, 1985c, p. 378). As Greene (1985) argues, once teachers engage with and recognize their own understandings, confrontations and lived reality, then they are able to project situations in which their students, in turn, are empowered to make sense of their lived situations. Indeed, once it has become possible to be clearer about the intellectual nature of teachers' labour – and of the critical, creative and insightful nature of what is required (Smyth, 1987) in order to develop in children the kinds of skills necessary to be able to enact active roles as citizens in a democracy (and not to be mere technicians or civil servants) – then 'the concept of intellectual [becomes] the basis for interrogating the specific ideological and economic conditions under which intellectuals as a group need to work in order to function as critical, creative human beings' (Giroux, 1985a, p. 28).

A CRITICAL RE-IMAGINING OF TEACHING

I don't want to dwell excessively or pessimistically on this, but what is clearly being constructed through these neo-liberal manoeuvres is an identity of the 'preferred' teacher – one who is dutiful, compliant, market responsive and uncritical of the circumstances and conditions around her – especially in respect of what the neo-liberal agenda is doing to schooling and groups within it.

The point I have been making thus far is that, at its essence, what neo-liberalism does is hand the process of the allocation of resources and their regulation (and by implication, 'life chances') over to the market to sort out – and where there is no market, it constructs a fake version of one. The net effect is that the stronger and more advantaged groups in these circumstances are able to take further advantage of their positionality. To put it more bluntly, already 'advantaged' students, their schools, families and communities benefit even more opportunistically, while those who have been *put at* a disadvantage because of their circumstances, exclusion or marginalization, and who are struggling to make sense of or to utilize available schooling, are rendered even moreso by dint of their alleged 'deficits'.

The underlying issue at stake here is the neutering of teachers and the way it renders them apolitical and non-partisan in a culture that says loudly and clearly that success is based solely upon meritocratic effort and that social and economic rewards come to those who make the investment of personal effort and who make appropriate choices. In other words, the message to teachers is that they ought not to have a 'social justice' agenda (or a socially critical one), nor should they be advocates for 'underdog' groups – questioning systems, structures or how things came to be the way they are is not considered to be part of the agenda of 'technicians'. Their role is to implement decisions, follow directions and not to question!

One of the pillars of the neo-liberal project as it has unfolded within education is the notion of 'evidence-based research' and its

29

concomitant 'evidence-based policy' – or as it has been labelled in the United States, 'scientific research'. In essence, this is about the idea that knowledge only exists if it has been legitimated by means of randomized, controlled experimental research approaches. In other words, research methods of the kind used in scientific laboratories – mostly on rats! This is the 'gold standard' mostly genuflected to by governments who regard this as the approach that ought to be used in all fields of discovery and investigation.

Nothing could be further from reality than the pursuit of this kind of research in the conflicted, confounded and complex social, political and economic realities of people's lives, aspirations and experiences in schools and communities – especially those disfigured and ravaged by international, corporate and predatory capitalism.

This model of research is really underpinned by a diseased way of thinking – all that needs to be done, so the thinking goes, is to diagnose the pathology, isolate it, determine the genetic make-up of the diseased bit and correct it by targeting an intervention, and magically the defect or deficiency will be fixed. If only it were so simple for social phenomenon!

This is a paradigm that is clearly grossly inappropriate to education, and it needs to be robustly confronted, dislodged, jettisoned and supplanted with a view of research on the work of teachers and teaching that is more in tune with schools and communities as social places.

There are a number of quite useful forms this re-imagining might take – for example, teacher-as-bricoleur (Huberman, 1983; 1988; 1990; Hatton, 1988; 1997; Smyth, 1995a; Honan, 2004; 2006), teacher-as-improviser (Erickson, 1982; Connell, 1996; Sawyer, 2001; 2004; Smyth et al., 2003), and teacher-as-social activist (Carlson, 1987; O'Loughlin, 1994; Roberts, 1997; Sachs, 2000; 2002; Avis, 2005; Perlstein, 2005). Each of these, to varying degrees, have their merits in the way they push back into the dominant 'evidence-based' thrust. This means pursuing a sharper and more politically focused imaging of teaching.

TEACHERS AS INTELLECTUALS/POLITICAL ACTORS

The notion that perhaps teachers are more than mindless technical operatives has been expressed widely and forcefully going back to Dewey and earlier. But, as Warham (1993) noted, no matter how vigorously one tries to escape it, teaching is by nature a political activity, both inside the classroom and outside of it, by virtue of those forces trying to make it otherwise. She argues that in order for a theory of teaching to be viable, it must acknowledge this undeniable fact.

Probably more than any other contemporary educator Giroux (1988) has championed the cause of teachers as intellectuals and the political ramifications of this cause. Giroux's extensive writings have occurred against a backdrop of educational reforms that have aimed to reduce teachers to 'the status of low-level employees or civil servants whose main function seems to be to implement reforms decided by experts in the upper levels of state and educational bureaucracies' (Giroux, 1985a, p. 20). The consequence, Giroux argues, is that the search and the push for technical/administrative solutions to the complex economy/society/ education linkage has produced a growing gulf between those who decide on technical and methodological grounds what is best for schools and the schools and teachers who deal with students, curriculum and pedagogy on a daily basis. He notes that there is a process of subjugation of intellectual labour at work here that in many cases reduces teachers to the 'status of high level clerks implementing the orders of others . . . or to the status of specialized technicians' (p. 21).

This dominance of technocratic rationality has produced a form of proletarianization of teachers' work not dissimilar to what happened to factory workers in the nineteenth century, as the control of what had previously been highly independent craftsman increasingly came under corporate and factory control. But, as Giroux (1985a) argues, what has occurred in schooling is more than just an elevation of the importance of the technical and the economic in the everyday life of schools:

> Underlying this technical rationality and its accompanying rationalization of reason and nature [has been] a call for the separation of conception from execution, the standardization of knowledge in the interests of managing and controlling it, and the devaluation of critical intellectual work for the primacy of practical considerations. (p. 23)

In a similar vein, teacher education has, Giroux says, all too often been reduced to questions of 'what works' (see US Department of Education, 1986; and Berliner and Biddle, 1995 for a critique). Issues regarding what counts as knowledge, what is worth teaching and how one judges the purpose and nature of teaching have thus become submerged (or even obliterated) in the press for routinization and standardization through what Giroux terms 'management pedagogies'.

Giroux's claim regarding how to rethink and restructure teachers' work is to view teaching as being able to 'illuminate and recover the rather general notion that all human activity involves some form of thinking [and] no activity, regardless of how routinized it might become, is abstracted from the functioning of the mind in some capacity' (Giroux, 1985a, p. 27). Applying this notion to teaching, Kohl (1983) stated,

> I believe a teacher must be an intellectual as well as a practitioner . . . I don't mean an intellectual in the sense of being a university professor or having a PhD . . . I am talking about activities of the mind. We must think about children, and create many philosophies of life in the classroom. (p. 30)

Kohl's (1983) argument is that unless teachers themselves make theories and test them, theories will be made for them by researchers and other groups only too willing to move in and fill 'the vacuum that teachers have created by . . . giving up their responsibility as intellectuals' (p. 30).

The kinds of questions Giroux (1985b) suggests are necessary if teachers are to interrogate their work so as to become intellectuals include the following:

- What counts as school knowledge?
- How is such knowledge selected and organized?
- What are the underlying interests that structure the form and content of school knowledge?
- How is what counts as school knowledge transmitted?
- How is access to such knowledge determined?
- What cultural values and formations are legitimated by dominant forms of school knowledge?
- What cultural formations are disorganized and delegitimated by dominant forms of school knowledge? (p. 91)

Teachers therefore need to be political actors in their educational settings in the sense of being clear about the different ways in which they experience their work – how they encounter it, how they understand it and how they feel about it (Ginsburg, 1988, p. 363). Adopting a political stance to one's work does not mean being a political partisan; it involves what Popkewitz (1987) describes as 'critical intellectual work'. Here, 'critical' means moving outside the assumptions and practices of the existing order and struggling to make categories, assumptions and practices of everyday life problematic (p. 350). But, as Ginsburg (1988) argues, it is more than just problematizing the work of teaching, because it involves the 'struggle to challenge and transform the structural and cultural features we . . . come to understand as oppressive and anti-democratic' (pp. 363–5). Ginsburg's point is that teachers need to see themselves as actively participating in progressive movements committed to bringing about fundamental social change (Anyon, 2005). According to this view, the image of teachers as compliant, passive and easily molded workers is replaced by a view of the teacher 'as an active agent, constructing perspectives and choosing actions' (Feiman-Nemser and Floden, 1986, p. 523).

The construal of teaching as a form of intellectual labour is one in which teachers regard their own classrooms and schools as sites of serious inquiry, with questions being asked and answered as to what schooling is about, how it works for some students and what conditions act to exclude others. This view of teaching is political in the sense that teachers do not take the nature of their work for granted (see Carlson and Apple, 1998) – they are prepared to question how it came to be that way and what sustains and maintains this set of views.

This has several dramatic and direct implications for students. The most obvious is a bringing of student lives, perspectives, cultures and experiences into the center of the curriculum in a way that involves students as co-constructors and co-creators (rather than passive consumers) of that curriculum, along with teachers. This preparedness of teachers and schools to take students' lives seriously means that the hierarchically scripted curriculum has to be modified (if not totally jettisoned) in order to accommodate the storied and narrative representations of the way students lead their increasingly complex lives (see, e.g., Ayers et al., 1998). This undermining means that issues previously off limits will have to be brought to centre stage and confronted in the classroom – issues such as racism, homophobia, gender, violence, poverty and economic exploitation. It will also mean that students will be more prominent, through, for example, researching the contexts and communities in which they live, unmasking questions that are usually marginalized or pushed off the social and educational agenda of schooling. Thus as teachers embrace the political in their work, a fundamental shift will occur in the direction of the genuine sharing of power with students, in ways that go considerably beyond many current inauthentic and tokenistic attempts.

PROBLEMATIZING APPROACHES TO TEACHING

To problematize teaching involves challenging habits and methods taken for granted and questioning fundamental and cherished assumptions. This usually occurs through a collective and collaborative process of teachers working with one another, examining and interrogating their teaching with probing questions such as the following:

- What is happening here?
- Who says this is the way things ought to happen?
- Who is it that is defining the work of teaching?
- How is that definition being fought over and resisted in various ways?
- What concessions and accommodations are being made?
- How are issues of skill, competency, professionalism and autonomy being expressed in the social relations of teaching?
- Whose interests are being served in the change process?
- What new forms of power are being used to focus power relations in teaching?
- How are the re-defined labor relations of teaching being played out? (Smyth, 1995a, p. 85)

Additional questions include the following:

- What overall purposes are being served?
- Whose vision is it anyway?
- Whose interests are being served?
- Whose needs are being met?
- Whose voices are being excluded, silenced, denied?
- How come some viewpoints always get heard?

- Why is this particular initiative occurring now?
- What alternatives have or should have been considered?
- What kind of feasible and prudent action can we adopt?
- Who can we enlist to support us?
- How can we start now?
- How are we going to know when we make a difference? (Smyth, 1995b)

Questioning of this kind moves significantly beyond examining teaching in limited individualistic frames or exclusively in terms of personal deficits (either of teachers or children). The starting point might be instances of classroom activity that are perplexing, confusing or troublesome; the intention is to locate or situate these in relation to wider change forces.

As long as attempts to improve teaching continue to be couched solely in terms of perceived individual deficits within teachers' pedagogical repertoires and styles (or the learning styles of students), then the process of improving teaching will fail to grapple systematically with historical and structural factors that make teaching (and learning) the way it is. Constructing problems as individual deficits also obscures the class, race and gender blindness of curricula and hence wider understandings of how power is exercised and in whose interests.

To problematize teaching is to adopt a 'critical' approach, by which I mean the posture of 'a certain skepticism, or suspension of assent, towards [an] . . . established norm or mode of doing things' (McPeck, 1981, p. 6). According to Garrison (1991), acting critically involves not taking things for granted, but it must also involve a constructive, positive and proactive aspect of allowing for alternative possibilities through 'a search for a more satisfactory insight or resolution of a troubling situation' (p. 289). Cox (1980) defined critical 'in the sense that it stands apart from the prevailing order of the world and asks how that order came to be' (p. 230).

Viewing teaching problematically involves raising doubts about the existing state of affairs. In the context of the classroom, a critical stance means raising questions about how the wider social context shapes and informs what goes on, through questions such as the following:

- Who talks in this classroom?
- Who gets the teacher's time?
- How is ability identified and attended to here, and what's the rationale?
- How is the unequal starting points of students dealt with here?
- How are instances of disruptive behavior explained and handled?
- Is there a competitive or a co-operative ethos in this classroom?
- Who helps who, here?
- Who's ideas are the most important or count most?
- How do we know that learning is occurring, here?
- Are answers or question more important in this classroom?
- How are decisions made here?
- How does the arrangement of the room help or hinder learning?
- Who benefits and who is disadvantaged in this classroom?
- How is conflict resolved?
- How are rules determined?
- How are inequalities recognized and dealt with?
- Where do learning materials come from?
- By what means are resources distributed?
- What career aspirations do students have, and how is that manifested?
- Who determined standards, and how are they arrived at?
- How is failure defined, and to what is it ascribed? Who or what fails?
- Whose language prevails in the classroom?
- How does the teacher monitor his/her agenda?

- How does the teacher work to change oppressive structures in the classroom?
- What is it that is being measured and assessed in this classroom?
- Who do teachers choose to work with collaboratively, on what, and under what circumstances? (Smyth, 1995b)

Developing ways of 'extraordinarily re-experiencing the ordinary' (Shor, 1980, p. 37) involves posing questions like 'why are we doing this?' and 'where will it get us?' This might involve disturbing and uncovering the way domination acts in our daily lives and becoming increasingly vigilant about the contradictions we live.

For example, Connell (1994) has shown that 'Australian schools deliver massive advantages to the children of the well-off and well-educated parents, and massive disadvantages to children of the poor and the poorly educated' (p. 1). That schools produce these effects over long time periods shows that such circumstances 'are not accidental, and they cannot be eliminated by minor tinkering with the system. It is clear that our education system is designed in a way that delivers "success" along lines of social and economic privilege. The way school knowledge is defined, and school learning is organized, has this effect' (p. 1). The consequence is that whereas education produces success for the privileged, education overall as a social institution fails – because the moral nature of the enterprise converts teachers into 'gatekeepers of privilege' implementing a curriculum that 'narrows the immense possibilities of learning' (p. 1). This tendency is exacerbated by the already well-advanced moves towards privatizing public education brought on by the exhortation to teachers, students and schools to compete against one another. This is a recipe for social stratification, segmentation and alienation.

Connell (1998) points to the Competitive Academic Curriculum' (CAC), with its 'abstract division of knowledge into "subjects"; a hierarchy of subjects; a hierarchical ordering of knowledge within each subject; a teacher-centered classroom-based pedagogy; an individualized learning process; [and] formal competitive assessment (the "exam")' (p. 84). This curriculum is constructed and implemented in ways that serve the interests of the *most* advantaged students while failing to value the experiences, speech, ideas and skills of students from the most disadvantaged groups in society. In other words, instead of constituting some set of common learning for all students, the CAC acts as a device for selecting those students whose largely middle-class backgrounds and experiences coincide with what is considered valuable and worthwhile knowledge. For the remaining students, mostly from minority and disadvantaged groups whose life experiences and cultures differ dramatically from the dominant (mostly male, Anglo, middle class), the effect is subordination, marginalization and eventually failure (Connell, 1993).

Connell (1994) argues the need to move beyond compensatory approaches for targeted groups, working instead for positive social justice at the grass-roots level, through posing questions and pursuing action around the following:

- What way of organizing learning and teaching will most benefit the least advantaged?
- What concept of teacher professionalism will most benefit the least advantaged?
- How can we democratize the relationship between public schools and working-class communities?
- How can we redefine the relationships between schools and other public and cultural institutions? (p. 2)

Questions like these require confronting the oppressive nature of individualism in society and seeing that students actually come from social groups. But at the moment, schools and classrooms are deeply entrenched in a pervasive ideology that frames modes of thinking and acting exclusively in terms of measurement and assessment, school discipline and behaviour management, competencies, standards and the like. Moving outside of this frame requires teachers who are able to uncover the dominant fallacy that 'individuals are autonomous and [therefore] responsible for making their own way', and that failure is something that can therefore be 'attributed to personal not social causation' (Razack, 1993, p. 49). The individual rights model does not offer any conceptual tools for understanding oppression and the systems that constrain individual choice. The model for positive social justice therefore shifts the focus to the systemic processes that block opportunities for groups by exposing the inadequacy of individual rights models for explaining what occurs in classrooms.

Teachers therefore need to work in ways that challenge what is taken for granted in their teaching and operate from the position that there may be other more just, inclusive and democratic ways that overcome various forms of classroom disadvantage. This means a preparedness by teachers to challenge the status quo (Smyth et al., 1998).

TEACHING FOR SOCIAL RESPONSIBILITY AND AGAINST THE GRAIN

Kreisberg (1992) helpfully highlights the central issue in classrooms as being how to convert the 'power of position' into the 'expertise of authority'. He says doing this requires questioning:

> What would an education based on dialogue and empowerment look like across cultures with their various ways of engaging in talk and learning? What would it mean to take democracy seriously in our daily lives? What kinds of relationships must exist among teachers so that they can respond directly and forcefully to racism, sexism and other forms of fascism, and the violence they bring, without simultaneously disempowering others? What are the possibilities for dialogue

in a society that seems to value 'talking at' more than 'talking with'? (p. 212)

For Kreisberg (1992), the major obstacle is the 'coercive character of schooling, and in particular the traditional power of the teacher' (p. 154). Relationships of domination saturate what occurs in schools, and the greatest challenge lies in developing in teachers the capacity to enter into 'power with relationships' with their students. Achieving this may be extraordinarily difficult, because the lived relationships of teachers – the way they think about themselves and how they connect to other teachers – may itself constitute a major form of domination.

Warham (1993) cast some light on what she regards as teachers employing dominant strategies when they use ritual language, routines to control large groups, loud tones of voice, non-verbal communication to control or assert power, and manipulating the structure of classroom discourses to exclude certain students (p. 214). On the other hand, teachers use less dominant strategies when they utilize peer-group pressure, encourage students, establish protracted eye contact, manipulate classroom discourse to support and include children, encourage positive thinking, ask favours, create group coherence, restate what children say when they lose track of the discourse, keep quiet and allow children to take responsibility for a discussion, engage in acts of politeness and kindness, make suggestions, praise and provide compliments, and enjoy humour (p. 214).

Classroom power, however, is never unidirectional; it is always two-way and dialectical, with resistance (in varying degrees) from and by students. When students use dominant strategies on their teachers they do not pay attention, yawn and show disinterest, demand attention, do not listen to their teacher, fiddle and distract other children, shuffle and become restless, and disobey the teacher's instructions (p. 215). When students use less dominant power strategies on the teacher they establish protracted eye contact, smile, enjoy humour, cooperate, listen carefully, and obey instructions (p. 215). Within and between the kind of spaces alluded to, it becomes clear that learning is not what the teacher/school/system requires that students do, so much as it is a negotiated process 'of what the children will allow the teacher to do' (Warham, 1993, p. 215).

Zeichner (1992) argues that in terms of barriers to teachers operating critically, there is much in the educational literature that amounts to 'bogus teacher development' (p. 3) that prevents teachers from asking 'questions related to the broader purpose of education in a democratic society' (p. 3). Continuing to perpetuate 'isolation of individual teachers and the lack of attention to the social context of teaching' (p. 9) means that this 'individualist bias makes it less likely that teachers will be able to confront and transform those structural aspects of their work that hinder the accomplishment of their educational mission' (p. 8). Zeichner is illustrative of someone who seeks to engage teachers with questions about how their 'everyday actions challenge or support various oppressions and injustices related to social class, race, gender, sexual preference, religion and numerous other factors.' (p. 12). His point is that we cannot assume the willingness of teachers to educate everyone's children, and unless teachers, even innovative ones, develop a commitment 'to the quality of relationships' and work to ensure that 'everybody's knowledge and cultural heritage is represented', then 'many students will continue to be bypassed by innovative school practices and continue to be denied, with the complicity of the school, access to decent and fulfilling lives' (p. 12). While it is unacceptable, he says, for teaching to be reduced to 'only its political elements' (p. 14), it is equally unacceptable for issues of equity and social justice to be relegated to the category of being other people's problems outside of the classroom.

Cochran-Smith (1991) and Simon (1992) have also pursued the idea that in order to bring about change through teaching it is necessary that teachers place themselves in situations in which they work against and challenge established norms. For Simon, the essence of changing teaching lies in trying not to succumb to pressures to rigidly encase notions like 'critical pedagogy' within definitions or procedures, but rather to see them as being reference points for 'an ongoing project and certainly not a prescriptive set of practices' (p. xvi). Simon presumes that 'teachers are cultural [and political] workers' and, as such, they engage in a process of helping students, 'challeng[ing] and assess[ing] existing social conventions, modes of thought, and relations of power' (p. 35) and arriving at conclusions about how situations came to be the way they are. He therefore admits to having a political vision that structures his work, that embraces questions such as

> How is experience to be understood? What information and experience do I have access to that is important and possibly helpful to others? In what way does the form and substance of the knowledge engaged in teaching situations enable/constrain personal and social possibilities? How do I understand learning and the relationship teaching has to it? What is my view of a 'person'? How do emotions, desires, and psychic investments influence teaching situations? How do the oppressive forms of power in my community manifest themselves in classrooms, and how do I situate myself in relation to such forms? And finally, how do I define my responsibilities as a teacher – to what should my students be held accountable, and to what should I be held accountable? (p. xvi)

Simon is seeking to offer 'a critical yet constructive way of reconstituting educational practice' (p. 5). All the while he keeps in mind, in the best tradition of self-reflection, that his own experiences as a teacher are continually woven into his 'participation in existing relations of domination' (p. 6). By focusing on his own contradictions, he can come to 'know where there is work yet to be done' (p. 6).

Cochran-Smith (1991) claims that what distinguishes schools and teachers who work 'against the grain' from others is their strong commitment to interrupting conservative influences and developing structures that produce 'critical dissonance' and 'collaborative resonance' (p. 304). That is to say, they generate 'intensification of opportunities to learn from teaching through the co-labor of communities' (p. 304) that focus on how school participants themselves might begin to 'bear upon the institutional and instructional arrangements of schooling' (p. 282). The process of collaborative resonance involves teachers in 'critiqu[ing] the cultures of teaching and schooling, research[ing] their own practices, articulat[ing] their own expertise, and call[ing] into question the policies and language of schooling that are taken for granted' (p. 283).

Teaching for social responsibility, as it comes through in the writing of people like Kriesberg, Zeichner, Simon and Cochran-Smith, underscores aspects such as the following:

- converting positional power into expertise of authority
- teachers working through dialogue with students
- teachers fostering forms of teaching that transcend dominance
- asking questions about the broader purpose of teaching
- moving outside of isolated teaching arrangements
- engaging with questions about how everyday teaching supports injustices and oppression
- assisting students to challenge existing social conventions and arrangements
- above all, having a moral vision for schooling.

TEACHING FOR DEMOCRACY AND SOCIAL JUSTICE

Engaging students with the big questions that fire the imagination and the forces that shape their lives is what Wood (1990) regards as the hallmark of a socially critical teacher. For example, in areas of high unemployment, teachers 'as curriculum workers' might engage their students with questions such as 'what work is here?; why are there no industries?; how can we get higher unemployment benefits?' (Wood, 1990, p. 98) While questions such as these do not have ready answers, they are a starting point for students to see beyond victim-blaming responses to what is occurring. In these ways, Wood's agenda is to have teachers develop critical forms of literacy which involve students in 'the ability to evaluate what is read or heard with respect to the interest being served' (Wood, 1988, p. 178). In particular, 'critical literacy involves building reading skills around students' own reading agendas. Having them read about things in which they have an interest and helping them write their own reading material are key components in this process' (p. 178). Viewed in this way, the curriculum, Wood (1990) argues, becomes 'shared – not . . . something that teachers dispense the way physicians prescribe medicine. Curriculum is a process in which teachers and students engage to order and make sense of the world' (p. 107).

Through the practices of Harmony School, Goodman (1992) highlights the tension between 'individuality' and 'community' as the school sought to rework what was meant by the notion of critical democracy. The experiences of Harmony show the importance of enabling students to acquire a connectionist perspective towards power that is tied to 'increasing their sense of social responsibility'. Goodman argues that the reciprocity that comes with power is crucial to its democratic enactment. The struggle is between a societal ethos of competitive individualism and a school that is trying to develop a collective sense of caring and a commitment to shared responsibility. Goodman's 'connectionist' view of power rests upon the claim that students must be given genuine opportunities to negotiate successfully with their teachers and that, in the process, teachers must be put 'at the center of the curriculum'. This is a far cry from worldwide moves at the moment to re-centralize control over schools, to colonize the curriculum, to narrow the curriculum through uniformity and to turn schools into institutions preoccupied with cultural production and mindless vocational training of the worst kind. The central organizing image Goodman describes is the importance of 'community' in schooling. It is the 'dialectical tension' between an atomistic society, on the one hand, and one characterized by social conformity, on the other, and it is the tendency for these to get out of balance that is crucial. Goodman's highlighting of how individualism reaches deep into American culture makes it easier to comprehend the significance of the attempt by teachers, administrators, parents and students at Harmony to work 'against the grain'.

One of the recurring themes coming through Goodman's book is that while teachers at Harmony mostly had a well-developed sense of caring and social responsibility in the way they worked with their students, they had been untouched by the forms of critical theorizing emanating from the academy. This is both understandable and explainable given the genre and the terrain upon which the largely academic debate has occurred. The difficulty for schools like Harmony is in the lack of connectedness to wider arenas of struggle outside of schools (see Anyon, 2005). This may be due in part to the need for those of us outside of schools to find better ways of 'adopting' practitioners in schools and working with them to better theorize the essence of what is occurring in schools. Goodman's description of what was being attempted at Harmony school, rather than providing a recipe to be followed, acts more as a beacon to work towards. Notions of democratic schooling are not forms of dogma to be blindly followed or transferred from one setting to another; rather, they are social, cultural and political constructions that reflect the way in which people inside schools choose to live their lives as students, teachers, administrators and parents.

Critical teaching for democracy and social justice can take many forms and shapes, and we need to not lose sight of what these approaches mean, practically speaking, for students. The following is an extended example of what this might look like. Bigelow (1998), a US classroom teacher, has his students look 'Behind the labels, the global sweatshop, Nike, and the race to the bottom':

> I began the lesson with a beat-up soccer ball. The ball sat balanced on a plastic container in the middle of the circle of student desks. 'I'd like you to write a description of this soccer ball,' I told my high school Global Studies class. 'Feel free to get up and look at it. There is no right or wrong. Just describe the ball however you'd like.'
>
> Looks of puzzlement and annoyance greeted me. 'It's just a soccer ball,' someone said . . . 'I'm not asking for an essay,' I said, 'just a paragraph or two.'
>
> As I'd anticipated, their accounts were straightforward – accurate if uninspired. Few students accepted the offer to examine the ball up close. A soccer ball is a soccer ball. They sat and wrote. Afterwards, a few students read their descriptions aloud. Brian's is typical: 'The ball is a sphere which has white hexagons and black pentagons. The black pentagons contain red stars, sloppily outlined in silver . . . one of the hexagons contains a green rabbit wearing a soccer uniform with "Euro 88" written parallel to the rabbit's body. This hexagon seems to be cracking. Another hexagon has the number 32 in green standing for the number of patches that the ball contains.'
>
> But something was missing. There was a deeper social reality associated with this ball – a reality that advertising and the consumption-oriented rhythms of U.S. daily life discouraged the students from considering. 'Made in Pakistan' was stenciled in small print on the ball, but very few students thought that significant enough to include in their descriptions. However, these three tiny words offered the most important clue to

the human lives hidden in 'just a soccer ball' – a clue to the invisible Pakistanis whose hands crafted the ball sitting in the middle of the room. (pp. 21–2)

After some discussion about their writing and after reading a poem to reorient them, Bigelow invited his students to 'resee' the soccer ball:

If you like, you can write from the point of view of the ball, you can ask the ball questions, but I want you to look at it deeply. What did we miss the first time around? It's not 'just a soccer ball'. With not much more than these words for guidance – although students had some familiarity with working conditions in poor countries – they drew the line beneath their original descriptions and began again.

Versions one and two were like night and day . . . Pakistan as the country of origin became more important. Tim wrote in part: 'Who built this soccer ball? The ball answers with "Pakistan". There are no real names, just labels. Where did the real people go after it was made?' Nicole also posed questions: 'If this ball could talk, what kinds of things would it be able to tell you? It would tell me about the lives of the people who made it in Pakistan . . . But if it could talk, would you listen?' . . . And Sarah imagined herself as the soccer ball worker. 'I sew together these shapes of leather. I stab my finger with my needle. I feel a small pain, but nothing much because my fingers are so callused. Everyday I sew these soccer balls together for 5 cents, but I've never once had a chance to play soccer with my friends. I sew and sew all day long to have these balls shipped to another place where they represent fun. Here, they represent the hard work of everyday life.' When students began to consider the human lives behind the ball-as-object, their writing also came alive . . . Students had begun to imagine the humanity inside the ball; their pieces were vivid and curious. The importance of making the visible the invisible, of looking behind the masks presented by everyday consumer goods, became the central theme of my first-time effort to teach about the 'global sweatshop' and child labor in poor countries. (pp. 22–3)

Needless to say, Bigelow was unsuccessful in getting the nearby representative from Nike to come and dialogue with his students. But he did have his students engage in a 'global clothes hunt' – bringing items of clothing or toys from hone (T-shirts, pants, skirts, shoes, Barbie dolls, baseball bats, etc.) to do an analysis of where the items were made and what sense the students made of this. He displayed their maps and collages and had the class search for patterns regarding where the goods were produced:

Some students noticed that electronic toys tended to be produced in Taiwan or Korea; that more expensive shoes, like Doc Martens, were manufactured in Great Britain or Italy; athletic shoes were made mostly in Indonesia or China. On their 'finding patterns' write up, just about everyone commented that China was the country that appeared most frequently on people's lists. A few kids noted that most of the people in the manufacturing countries were not white. As Sandee wrote, 'The more expensive products seemed to be manufactured in countries with a higher number of white people. Cheaper products are often from places with other than white' . . . We'd spent the early part of the year studying European colonialism, and some students noticed that many of the manufacturing countries were former colonies. I wanted students to see that every time they put clothes on or kick a soccer ball they are making a connection, if hidden, with people around the world – especially in the Third World – and that these countries are rooted in historical patterns of global inequality. (p. 28)

Bigelow's examples beautifully capture the essence of what is involved in critical teaching emerging from everyday life. This perspective can be summarized as follows:

- teachers engaging students with questions that have relevance beyond the classroom
- working with students in ways that enable them to delve more deeply into content that is normally presented to them
- schools and teachers operating in other than individual and competitive ways, and creating forms of shared responsibility and community
- changing mindsets and orientations rather than using 'how-to-do-it' approaches
- listening to voices that originate from within classrooms
- using personal experience as a starting point and source of knowledge
- questioning the authority of the teacher as the sole source of knowledge
- students themselves becoming important alternative sources of theorizing about learning
- focusing on how power is reproduced through structures and forms of language
- encouraging the translation of democratic processes pursued inside the classroom into venues outside.

CRITICAL TEACHING AND CRITICAL PEDAGOGY IN THE CLASSROOM

Shor's *Critical Teaching and Everyday Life* (1980) and *When Students Have Power* (1996) explore ways of democratizing social relations in the classroom that are indicative of what it means to operate in dialogical ways. He shows how sources within our culture interfere with critical thought. His starting point is schooling as a social practice in which 'dialogue is a democratic model of social relations, used to probematize the undemocratic quality of social life' (p. 95).

Bigelow (1990, 1992) pursues a similar agenda in creating a classroom which becomes 'part of a protracted argument for the viability of a critical and participatory democracy' (1992, p. 19). Bigelow seeks to get his students to see how society reproduces inequalities. He does this through a 'dialogical' approach to teaching in which he has his students critique the larger society by probing the social factors that make and limit their lives, who they are, and who they *could* be (pp. 19–20). Bigelow's concern is to confront the dynamics of power and the role of resistance – in other words, learning about the 'causes for their own insubordination, [and] the role they could play . . . in resisting it' (p. 22). Bigelow (1992) is clearly 'excited by this sociological detective work' (p. 22) in which he sees his own role as helping shape students' perceptions of the larger society.

Viewed in this way, schooling becomes a project of helping students to see injustices and assisting them both to locate themselves in relation to such issues and to see how society is structured in ways that both sustain and maintain those inequities. This necessarily involves working with students in ways that enable teachers to see, through their own pedagogical work in classrooms, how knowledge and power are inextricably linked and that students also need to see themselves as having a crucial role in 'problematizing knowledge, utilizing dialogue, and making knowledge meaningful so as to make it critical in order to make it emancipatory' (Giroux, 1985a, p. 87).

My own approaches (Smyth, 1991) in *Teachers as Collaborative Learners: Challenging Dominant Forms of Supervision* seek to engage teachers in recognizing and extirpating inappropriate pedagogies and ideologies. Instead of the toxic practices being pressed upon schools from the corporate sector that are producing such distortion and disfigurement, schools need coherent theories about teaching crafted by teachers themselves. I have envisaged a number of layered moments, summarized below (Smyth, 1993).

1. Describing

If teachers are to celebrate the virtues of their work, as well as convince others of its efficacy, then the starting point is to describe the situational specifics of their teaching. In this, teachers need the assistance of colleagues in looking for similarities, differences, patterns, regularities, discontinuities, contradictions and ruptures in their teaching. In a word, they need assistance in becoming 'informed' so as to see the theories in their teaching.

2. Informing

Other people's theories are often foisted onto teachers. But, given the opportunity of explaining the meaning that lies behind their teaching, teachers can be perceptive at unraveling the complexity of classrooms. They are thus able to unravel their teaching so as to exemplify local theories and gain a platform from which to make sense of their teaching as well as from which to explain it to others. No longer having to depend on others' theories also provides teachers with the courage to confront whoever is doing the defining, articulating and legitimating knowledge about teaching. The issue of who has the right to do these things can be confronted and therefore contested.

3. Confronting

Teachers can ascertain 'how things came to be this way' and what broader forces operate to make them like this biographically by pursuing questions such as the following:

- What do my teaching practices say about my assumptions, values and beliefs about teaching?
- What social practices are expressed in these ideas?

- What causes me to maintain my theories?
- What constrains my views of what is possible in teaching?

By the time teachers have begun to grapple with questions such as these and the forces that are shaping what they do, they are starting to think about how to act in different ways and are moving towards *reconstructing* parts of their teaching and the contexts and structures within which they teach.

The key thematic issues I have focused on through critical approaches to teaching and classroom pedagogy have included the following:

- asking critical questions as the major method by which teachers probe their teaching
- challenging passivity
- searching for interrelationships between narrated, storied accounts of teaching and the deeper meanings in teaching
- critiquing the everyday practice of teaching, as well as envisaging what alternatives might look like
- asking how teaching becomes unwittingly implicated in maintaining the status quo
- pursuing a number of moments or phases embracing elements of describing, informing, confronting, and reconstructing teaching.

CONCLUSION

The central point of this chapter has been that teaching for social responsibility, or acting in socially critical ways, is crucial in creating counter-hegemonic resistance to neo-liberalism. Schools are one of the few remaining social institutions that still have a capacity to enculturate the young in ways of organization that celebrate social relationships. Teachers are crucial agents in the process of asking questions that unmask the nature of teaching and learning and the interests being served or denied.

I have explored an issue that rarely gets coverage in debates about teaching and teachers' work – namely, teachers as social theorists and political actors. My broader purpose has been to illustrate how teaching might be construed so as to assist in the reclamation of a democracy of social responsibility and to engage teachers in investigating the practice, meaning and intent of what lies behind schooling. The central argument has been that for too long teachers have been treated in ways that deny the importance of teaching as a social practice – one concerned with teaching for social responsibility, democracy, social justice, connectedness and civility. Teachers' work has always been an avowedly political process, long characterized by decisions about what knowledge gets taught, and what gets omitted; whose view of the world is privileged, and whose is denied; what forms of pedagogy are inclusive, and which are exclusive; and whose interests are served, and whose are marginalized and excluded. These are no longer matters that should be spoken about in hushed tones, for it is clear that if teachers are not political about their work (in the sense of being critically reflective about it and the implications that has for the life chances of children), then they are the only group affiliated with teaching who operate in such allegedly detached ways.

CHAPTER 3

Students-as-Activists in Their Own Learning

When I invoke the term 'students as activists' I am not trying to conjure up images of students manning the barricades, rioting in the streets, throwing petrol bombs or forcibly occupying central educational offices. On the contrary, I have in mind an altogether different idea, one that is much closer to what Postman and Weingartner (1971) refer to as the 'soft revolution'. As they put it, the soft revolution has as its purpose the renewal and reconstruction of educational institutions without the use of violence' (p. 3).

The idea of the soft revolution is an idea worth pursuing for a moment both as a metaphor and as a political strategy. As Postman and Weingartner (1971) put it,

> The soft revolution is characterized by a minimum of rhetoric, dogma and charismatic leadership . . . It begins anywhere and anytime someone finds room enough to do something that is better than what's going on . . . The basic metaphor of a soft revolution is judo . . . When you are using judo, you do not oppose the strength of your adversary. You use your adversary's strength against himself, and in spite of himself (in fact, *because* of himself). (pp. 4–5)

The landscape of schools that Postman and Weingartner (1971) described in the 1970s could well be that existing in the second decade of the twenty-first century – except immeasurably worse. Nothing seems to have changed: schools are still intellectually and spiritually murdering almost everybody, and in spite of all the high-pitched noise, there is no decent 'game plan' to stop them (p. 6). Their argument is that bringing about radical change requires that people confront the existential realities within which they exist. What this means is that in order to get people to consider changing something, you have to get them to think about it. In order to get them to think about it, you have to make it visible to them (p. 80). In other words, the notion of the soft revolution is predicated on 'mak[ing] the ordinary visible' (p. 80). To bring about change in schools, what is considered to be ordinary, routine and habitual has to be made 'visible to those who unthinkingly accept it', and the way to do that 'is to interrupt it' (p. 80) – but more about the practicalities of this in a moment.

The kind of *soft revolution* this chapter addresses is one which humanizes schools so that they become more hospitable to the lives, interests, backgrounds and aspirations of young people (especially those from 'disadvantaged' or challenging contexts), rather than institutions of incarceration, fear, punishment and retribution. In order to bring on the kind of transformative pedagogy implicit in this kind of revolution, the starting point has to be sorting out some major philosophical questions, such as the difference between 'failure' and 'not learning' – and these are two fundamentally different concepts. Kohl (1994) captured this in the title of his book *I Won't Learn from You*. Kohl puts it like this:

> Failure is characterized by the frustrated will to know. Failure results from a mismatch between what the learner wants to do and is able to do. The reasons for failure may be personal, social, or cultural, but whatever they are, the results of failure are most often a loss of self-confidence accompanied by a sense of inferiority and inadequacy. Not-learning [on the other hand]

produces thoroughly different effects. It tends to strengthen the will, clarify one's definition of self, reinforce self-discipline, and provide inner satisfaction. Not-learning can also get one into trouble if it results in defiance or refusal to become socialized in ways that are sanctioned by the dominant authority. (p. 6)

The reason this distinction is so crucial in a high stakes area like education is that unless we are very clear about what we name as 'the problem', we end up perpetrating huge injustices in the way we come up with what purport to be the 'solutions'.

Kohl (1994) argues that

until we learn to distinguish not-learning from failure and to respect the truth behind this massive rejection of schooling by students from poor and oppressed communities, we will not be able to solve the major problems of education . . . Risk taking is at the heart of teaching well. That means that teachers will have to not-learn the ways of loyalty to the system and to speak out . . . We must give up looking at resistant students as failures. (p. 32)

Therefore the kinds of questions we have to have the courage to address and heroically speak out about are as follows:

- Who succeeds at school?
- Why does schooling work for these groups?
- Whose interests are being served by the institution of schooling?
- Who gets excluded, marginalized or 'failed' by the way schools are organized and enacted?
- How did things come to be this way, and what conditions support and sustain this situation?
- How can we go beyond individualizing the problem and pathologizing some groups, by labelling and targeting them as 'at risk'?

- How can we collectively confront power inequalities?
- How can we locate and use existing reservoirs of talent and ability in this school and its community?
- How can we do something for equity today, and with whom?
- Who are the people I turn to for ideas? (there are no gurus – only people like us!)
- How can we have less talk and more action? (Smyth, 2008)

What is at the heart of these questions, and the basis of the transformational reforms required, are questions about who schools exist for as they are currently configured and whose voices are predominantly listened to. These are questions that strike at the very centre of the current dominant managerialist view of schools – namely, that everything will be 'fixed' if schools are better managed, and that as a result they will do their economic work of improving the national skills base, enhancing economic competitiveness and facilitating the work of capitalism.

Asking questions like these and forcing answers leads us in the direction of making schools accountable to young people, who are their major 'stakeholders'. Pushing for these kind of interrogations creates circumstances in which alternatives are forced into existence – ones that are forged collaboratively and that involve young people themselves.

To take a particular illustration – the underlying principles and assumptions regarding the ways schools are organized and operated are so entrenched and accepted that nobody ever questions them. Here are eight of the major shibboleths that underpin school programs almost anywhere in the world (especially in relation to high schools):

(1) that knowledge is best presented and comprehended when organized into 'subjects,' (2) that most subjects have a specific 'content,' (3) that the content of these subjects is more or less stable, (4) that a major function of the teacher is to 'transmit'

this content, (5) that the most practical place to do this is in a room within a centrally located building, (6) that students learn best in 45-minute periods which meet five times a week, (7) that students are learning when they are listening to the teacher, reading their texts, doing their assignments, and otherwise 'paying attention' to the content being transmitted, and, finally, (8) that all of this must go on as preparation for life. (Postman and Weingartner, 1971, p. 9)

Now, these are an eminently interruptible set of propositions, especially when considered from the vantage point of young people. The kind of interruption that needs to occur to make these shibboleths visible involves positing a radically different set of views that go something like this:

(1) that learning takes place best *not* when it is conceived as a preparation for life, but when it occurs in the context of real daily life, (2) that each learner, ultimately, must organize [her] own learning in [her] own way, (3) that 'problems' and personal interests are a more realistic structure than are 'subjects' for organizing learning experiences, (4) that students are capable of directly and authentically participating in the intellectual and social life of their community, and (5) that the community badly needs them to do this. (Postman and Weingartner, 1971, p. 9)

Shor (1996) captured the essence of what needs to be pushed back into, and what I am calling *students as activists in their own learning*, in the title of his book *When Students Have Power*. Using his own experiences teaching a working-class group of students (although they did not describe themselves in these words) in a community college, Shor describes his attempt at power sharing with students in what Kreisberg (1992) calls 'power with' rather than 'power over'.

Shor (1996) draws upon Pratt's (1991) notion of 'contact zones' as a heuristic for analyzing the conflicted and conflictual territory between teachers and students. As Pratt (1991) puts it, a contact zone refers to 'social spaces where cultures meet, clash, and grapple with each other, often in contexts of highly asymmetrical relations of power' (p. 1) – and classrooms are a prominent example of this. What is deemed legitimate in classrooms 'is defined from the point of view of the party in authority – regardless of what other parties might see themselves as doing' (Pratt, 1991, p. 5). Viewed from this vantage point, the social world of the classroom 'tends to be described almost entirely from the point of view of the teacher and teaching, not from the point of view of pupils' (p. 5). If the social world of the classroom is analysed at all, it is as a 'unified and homogenized' one with respect to the teacher, and 'whatever the students do other than what the teacher specifies is invisible or anomalous to the analysis' (p. 5).

The way Shor (1996) puts it is that the kind of students he works with adapt within the contact zone 'through various means of accommodation and resistance . . . They appear to be rejecting authority and submitting to it at the same time' (p. 12). A classic illustration of this is the hypothetical student who says: 'Get fucked Miss, and you too, Sir!' The paradox ought to be evident enough here!

When students from non-middle-class backgrounds encounter the largely middle-class institution of schooling, there is bound to be 'interactive trouble' (Freebody et al., 1995). Shor (1996) says that these young people 'have internalized a political compass that compels them to go into . . . exile' (p. 16). Metaphorically speaking, 'They know me [the teacher, institutionally, and in terms of expected role] before they meet me' (p. 16). What he is saying is that these young people already have a well-rehearsed understanding of what kind of places schools are and how the various actors in them, themselves included, are expected to operate. They have been learning their subordinated place in school and society for considerable periods of time, 'and they reenact and reconstitute their marginality . . . [by occupying the] marginal space [from which] they can more easily resist the very process marginalizing them' (p. 15) – hence the simultaneous process of accommodating while resisting.

To illustrate what I am saying here,'they expect an authoritarian rhetorical setting: teacher talk, teacher-centered standard English, an official syllabus with remote subject matter, and unilateral rule making' (Shor, 1996, p. 16). So history is of crucial importance here, and any attempt to be democratic and inclusive is likely to be met with resistance, with 'students . . . constructing the subordinate self at the same time that they are resisting and undermining it, while believing that their "real selves", "real lives", are somewhere else, not contaminated or controlled by this dominating process' (Shor, 1996, p. 17). The paradox is that these 'students are actively constructing their apparent passivity and withdrawal, which is not really passive and not exactly withdrawn' (p. 16). Part of this conundrum can be explained if we understand the role that fear and insecurity play – even when groups like this are provided with what are demonstrably more supportive, democratic and inclusive sets of opportunities. These students

- don't want to share authority . . . it's more demanding to take responsibility';
- don't like the negotiating process' – [they would prefer to have] 'the expert tell them [what to do]';
- don't know how to use authority to negotiate [their learning]' because they have never had the experience before and have 'become authority-dependent';
- don't understand . . . power-sharing' discourses and can't make sense of it because of their subordinated history;
- don't trust [in the] sincerity [of] the negotiation process even if it appeals to them. . . because there is an extremely high level of

risk involved]. . . in taking an unknown road [especially] with a more powerful official stranger as a guide'; and

• are reluctant to take public risks by speaking up in an unfamiliar process'. (Shor, 1996, pp. 18–19)

CONTINUING THE ARGUMENT FOR *STUDENT VOICE*

As a precursor to a glimpse into a high school in extraordinarily difficult circumstances that had taken a few small provisional steps towards recasting itself in the direction of *students having a voice in their learning*, I want to briefly sculpt out the case for school reform that starts from a radically different place than where we are at currently.

If we want to understand how young people are disengaging and disconnecting from schools in alarming numbers, then we need to access what is going on from the inside out. In other words, we need to explore these issue from the standpoint or 'positional lenses' (Glazier, 2005) of the existential experiences of young people and, from there, begin to construct more feasible platforms from which to pursue forms of school organization, culture and leadership that acknowledge those important realities.

The reasons students withdraw from school emotionally, educationally, psychologically and eventually physically, are multifaceted and complex, but in the end they boil down to 'political' reasons – that is to say, students refuse to make the emotional and relational investment necessary to become engaged with the social institution of schooling in a manner necessary for learning to occur. Educational anthropologists such as Erickson (1987), Ogbu (1982) and Levinson (1992) make it clear that when young people withdraw (or even disengage) from schooling, they are resisting or withdrawing their assent. According to Erickson (1987), when we say students are 'not learning', and by implication when students choose to separate themselves from schooling, what we mean is that they are

> 'not learning' what school authorities, teachers and administrators intend for them to learn as a result of intentional instruction. Learning what is deliberately taught can be seen as a form of political assent. Not learning can be seen as a form of political resistance. (Erickson, 1987, pp. 343–4)

What is fundamentally at stake when students agree to learn in schools, Erickson (1987) argues, is the triumvirate of legitimacy, trust and interest – at the institutional as well as at an existential level. As he put it,

> Assent to the exercise of authority involves trust that its exercise will be benign. This involves a leap of faith – trust in the legitimacy of the authority and in the good intentions of those exercising it, trust that one's own identity will be maintained positively in relation to the authority, and trust that one's own interests will be advanced by compliance with the exercise of authority. (p. 344)

Where Erickson (1987) is leading us is towards the argument that students have (and are continually exercising) choices, and that these choices are played out in and through pedagogic relations created and sustained (in varying degrees) between teachers and students. He says that in this

> it is essential that the teacher and students establish and maintain trust in each other at the edge of risk . . . To learn is to entertain risk, since learning involves moving past the level of competence, which is already mastered, to the nearest region of incompetence, what has not yet been mastered. (p. 344)

Erickson (1987) is worth following a little further because of what he portrays as lying at the very heart of whether school is going to work or not for increasing numbers of non-middle-class students of colour in the United States and elsewhere. There are some extremely powerful clues in here as to what needs to be done in a policy and practice sense. Success and failure at school needs to be recast in multi-directional terms:

> To speak of school success or failure is to speak of learning or not learning what is deliberately taught there. Learning is ubiquitous in human experience throughout the life cycle, and humans are very good at it . . . Yet in schools, deliberately taught learning seems to be a problem. It is differentially distributed along lines of class, race, ethnicity, and language background. (p. 343)

Often what we do instead of this more robust version is to regard learning as being unidirectional, which is to say we allow it to be cast in transmission terms, rather than as an act of co-creation between teachers and students:

> The teacher tends to use clinical labels and to attribute internal traits to students (eg. 'unmotivated') rather than seeing what is happening in terms of invisible cultural differences. Nor does the teacher see student behavior as interactionally generated – a dialectical relation in which the teacher is inadvertently co-producing with students the very behavior that he or she is taking as evidence of an individual characteristic of the student. Given the power difference between teacher and student, what could be seen as an interactional phenomenon to which teacher and student both contribute ends up institutionalized as an official diagnosis of student deficiency. (Erickson, 1987, pp. 337–8)

What gets misunderstood in the process is the dialectical nature of school failure:

the reflexive way in which schools 'work at' failing their students and students 'work at' failing to achieve in school. School success is used in a similarly reflexive sense, as something the school does as well as what the student does. (Erickson, 1987, p. 336)

And what gets lost as a consequence is the crucial opportunity 'to consider school motivation and achievement as a political process in which issues of institutional and personal legitimacy, identity, and economic interest are central' (Erickson, 1987, p. 341). I have argued at some length elsewhere (Smyth et al., 2004), that school failure is inextricably bound up with the process of students doing 'identity work' (Snow and Anderson, 1987). Whether young people stay in school or not depends in part on the sense they make of themselves, their community and their future, and in part on 'the adaptive strategies they use to accept, modify, or resist the institutional identities made available to them' (Fraser et al., 1997, p. 222). In this sense, doing identity work involves a complex negotiation to maintain 'one's overarching view or image of her or himself as a physical, social, spiritual and moral being' (Snow and Anderson, 1987, p. 1348). This involves struggling to sustain a working compromise between the meaning individuals attribute to themselves and the social (or institutional) identities made available to them. In this sense, many young people are living multiple consciousnesses – living in one reality at home, in another reality with peers and then negotiating another reality at school. Many young people negotiate their lives through consciously taking on different identities in these different contexts (Gilroy, 1993).

Succeeding at school, for many students, means having to suppress their own identities and to act within a narrowly defined and institutionalized view of what it means to be a 'good' student. For many young people, going to school involves a particular and difficult type of identity work – negotiating/suppressing their own identities. Schools offer possibilities for future independence, and they

65

also offer conceptual resources that can contribute to some identities. The struggle over identity at school, however, can become too difficult to negotiate for some. For students who 'drop out', school has effectively lost its potential to contribute to their life plans. Schooling is no longer seen as a viable place in which to do identity work.

As I have demonstrated in my previous work on this topic (Smyth et al., 2004), rather than blaming social structures or 'blaming the victim', we need to understand early school leaving in terms of the process that gets to be played out in the relationship between young people and schools. What seems to be happening, as young people negotiate their lives in and around post-schooling, is a clash of frames of reference. The school operates with one frame of reference, or maybe more, but students bring their own frames of reference. Often schools assume a high degree of shared understanding of their frame of reference, an assumption that is often way off the mark. This misunderstanding is what Freebody et al. (1995) describe as 'interactive trouble' in situations characterized by breakdowns in communication. Such breakdowns occur when there is a lack of understanding by students of the cues within teacher talk, a failure by teachers to hear cues in student talk, an application of overly subtle criteria by teachers and a possible misreading by either the teacher or the students about what is going on in the context of the classroom. Interactive trouble names what is going on in the relationships between students and teachers. Interactive trouble is way of understanding what is happening when cultural discontinuities are given expression in the everyday experiences of school, its students and the curriculum.

To accord Erickson (1987) a final word, for the moment, on the issue of the way in which schools match (or not) cultural identities and whether they generate situations in which students acquiesce or withhold their assent to learn, thereby resisting what schools have on offer,

As students grow older and experience repeated failure and negative encounters with teachers, they develop oppositional cultural patterns as a symbol of their disaffiliation with what they experience . . . The more alienated the students become, the less they persist in doing schoolwork . . . The student becomes either actively resistant – seen as salient and incorrigible – or passively resistant – fading into the woodwork as an anonymous well-behaved, low-achieving student. (p. 348)

In other words, when students withdraw or disengage, they are developing and pursuing an 'oppositional identity' (p. 349) that is inconsistent to that being proffered by the school. Students refuse to accept the 'negative identity' assigned by the school 'by refusing to learn' (p. 350).

IMPLICATIONS FOR SCHOOL CULTURE, ORGANIZATION AND LEADERSHIP

There are no magic formulae, silver bullets, organizational charts, typologies of school culture or heroic formulations of leadership capable of rectifying this situation. At best, we can only hope to extricate ourselves by having the courage to ask profound questions about what we are doing in schooling. But that is ultimately what leadership is all about – a preparedness to challenge the status quo with alternatives.

If we are sincere about wanting to minimize the amount of negative identity formation and miscommunication between schools and their students that precipitates in failure for both, then we will have to be prepared to place much greater emphasis on putting relationships at the centre of everything schools do. But as Bryk and Schneider (2002) lament, 'there is relatively little acknowledgement of these relational concerns in either education policy or the more general education research literature' (p. 7). To invoke the shorthand of Bingham and Sidorkin's (2004) book, there is

No Education Without Relation, and to remedy this situation we will have to jettison our fetish with 'structural change' and 'governance reform' and their preoccupation with 'incentives and control mechanisms' (Bryk and Schneider, 2002, p. 4) and embrace instead the palpable reality that schools are places that have to do with personal dynamics that profoundly impact on whether students attend and learn. Practically speaking, this will depend on how power relations are acknowledged and exercised. If we are to accept that schools are principally relational organizations that are in the business of making available the social and institutional resources to enable young people to 'make' their identities, then the pressing question hinges around how schools are to do this. Bryk and Schneider (2002) advance our thinking on this crucial issue by arguing that 'relational trust' is a necessary institutional resource for learning, which is to say, giving students a voice and a say in what and how they learn. They put it like this: 'the social relationships at work in school communities comprise a fundamental feature of their operations. The nature of these social exchanges, and the local cultural features that shape them, condition and school's capacity to improve' (p. 5). Creating schools as 'learning organizations', to borrow from the current popular vernacular, is to have schools that invest students with 'relational power' (Warren, 2005). Relational power, in the sense in which Warren (2005) uses it, refers to the building of trust within and across a range of groups in schools in ways that enable the development and pursuit of a common vision about how schooling can work for all, including those most marginalized and excluded. It is about using the capacity that inheres in relationships to begin to address and redress social and structural inequality in terms of who succeeds and who fails. Relational power is a 'set of resources' in that it draws upon 'trust and cooperation between and among people' (Warren, 2005, p. 136) and acknowledges that learning involves 'the power to get things done collectively' (p. 138) by confronting, rather than denying, power inequalities.

When we fail to comprehend this in institutions like schools, what we fall prey to is what Sidorkin (2002) says routinely happens with politicians and educational policy makers who resort to a stimulus-response formulae, because 'the lack of a better theory forces them to fall back on behaviorist frameworks, crude but simple and appealing to the public. Thus talk of "accountability" and "consequences" permeates popular educational discourse' (pp. 81–2). The alternative is to start out from the position, as a teacher delightfully put it to me recently, of working to make students 'powerful people' – by which she meant relating to students in ways that conveyed to them a genuine sense that they really 'can do it' and working with them to cooperatively achieve this end. This means going beyond stigmatizing students from the most disadvantaged backgrounds as 'bundles of pathologies' (Saegert et al., 2001, cited in Warren, 2005, pp. 134–5) to be 'fixed up' and regarding them instead as having valuable resources and backgrounds.

When teachers and school leaders start by conveying to students the expectation that 'they can do it', what gets interrupted is the familiar cycle of failure, and in its place a situation of relational trust is constructed whereby an ensemble of pedagogical approaches and activities are brought into existence, committed to success. This is the antithesis of what Kozol referred to in an interview as the 'sociopathic' view of accountability in vogue through testing regimes, in which 'the driving motive is to highlight failure in inner-city schools as dramatically as possible in order to create a ground swell of support for private vouchers or other privatizing schemes' (Solomon, 2005, p. 14).

When we fail to place relationships at the centre of schooling and allow the experiences of increasing numbers of students to be degraded, corroded, fractured, fragmented and rendered meaningless, then we fail in one of our most fundamental responsibilities as citizens in a democracy. As Noddings (2005) has argued, by continuing to insist for no good reason on pursuing reductionist drill and practice approaches and high stakes testing, we have dramatically weakened our sense of community and trust in schools and replaced it with security guards, metal detectors and more surveillance cameras. Restoration of trust will involve having the courage to ask the question 'what social arrangements might reduce the need for such measures?' and to tackle the violence, alienation, ignorance and unhappiness in our schools by exploring more hopeful possibilities, such as the following:

> Smaller schools? Multiyear assignment of teachers and students? Class and school meetings to establish rules and discuss problems? Dedication to teaching the whole child in every class? Serious attention to the integration of subject matter? Gentle but persistent invitations to all students to participate? More opportunities to engage in the arts and in social projects? More encouragement to speak out with the assurance of being heard? More opportunities to work together? Less competition? Warmer hospitality for parents? More public forums on school issues? Reduction of test-induced stress? More opportunities for informal conversation? Expanding, not reducing, course offerings? Promoting the idea of fun and humor in learning? Educating teachers more broadly? All of the above? (Noddings, 2005, p. 12)

I want to illustrate what this looks like, practically speaking, by drawing upon Haberman's (1991) seminal paper 'The Pedagogy of Poverty Versus Good Teaching'. Speaking about the long-term, seemingly incorrigible problem of teaching non-middle-class students in urban schools (the ones most represented in the plethora of current statistics of students 'dropping out' of 'failing' high schools in the United States), Haberman argues that a particular teaching style has become even more solidified than when he first noted it back in 1958. What Haberman rehearses is an ensemble of now familiar pedagogical approaches that are domesticated, emaciated and totally devoid of educational richness or vitality. This has become 'the coin of the realm in urban schools' (p. 291) – not only because it constitutes what teachers do, but also because 'youngsters expect' it and because parents, the community and the general public are comforted by the fact that this is what teaching is unassailably assumed to be. To not being doing it 'would be regarded as deviant . . . [and] be considered prima facie evidence of not teaching' (p. 291), including such commonly identified teaching acts as the following:

- giving information
- asking questions
- giving directions
- making assignments
- monitoring seatwork
- reviewing assignments
- giving tests
- reviewing tests
- assigning homework
- reviewing homework
- settling disputes
- punishing noncompliance
- Marking papers, and
- Giving grades. (p. 291)

This is not to suggest that all of these activities are totally regressive, damaging or totally inappropriate – for clearly they are not, and some of them are eminently sensible, on occasion. What is problematic is when they are dogmatically prescribed and become the basis of professionally and fiscally punitive and retributive action. Even more worrying is when they are presented as if there were no alternatives. Haberman (1991) argues

71

with uncanny clarity, given the circumstances we are currently in, that what gives the pedagogy of poverty sustenance are people:

- . . . who themselves did not do well in schools. People who have been brutalized are usually not rich sources of compassion . . .
- . . . who rely on common sense rather than on thoughtful analysis. It is easy to criticize humane and developmental teaching aimed at educating a free people as mere 'permissiveness' . . .
- . . . who fear minorities and the poor. Bigots typically become obsessed with the need for control . . .
- . . . who have low expectations for minorities and the poor. People with limited vision frequently see value in limited and limiting forms of pedagogy. They believe that at-risk students are served best by a directive, controlling pedagogy . . .
- . . . who do not know the full range of pedagogical options available. This group includes most school administrators, most business and political reformers, and many teachers. (p. 291)

What follows logically and consistently from and 'undergird[s] the pedagogy of poverty' (p. 291) are a number of propositions that are proving difficult to shake that say,

1. Teaching is what teachers do. Learning is what students do. Therefore, students and teachers are engaged in different activities.
2. Teachers are in charge and responsible. Students are those who still need to develop appropriate behavior. Therefore, when students follow teachers' directions, appropriate behavior is being taught and learned.
3. Students represent a wide range of individual differences. Many students have handicapping conditions and lead debilitating home lives. Therefore, ranking of some sort is inevitable;

some students will end up at the bottom of the class while others will finish at the top.

4. Basic skills are a prerequisite for learning and living. Students are not necessarily interested in basic skills. Therefore, directive pedagogy must be used to ensure that youngsters are compelled to learn their basic skills. (p. 291)

These kind of refrains are uttered with such frequency and with such authority that they take on the mantle of an unchallengeable credo, but as Haberman (1991) notes,

> Unfortunately, the pedagogy of poverty does not work. Youngsters achieve neither minimum levels of life skills nor what they are capable of learning. The classroom atmosphere created by constant teacher direction and student compliance seethes with passive resentment that sometimes bubbles up into overt resistance. Teachers burn out because of the emotional and physical energy that they must expend to maintain their authority every hour of every day. (p. 291)

The very real danger here in the context of the shrill and incessant press to 'make students learn', both in their own self-interest and for the common good, is to operate in the belief that 'there must be a way to force students to work hard enough to vindicate the methodology' (p. 292), or put another way, to 'act as if it is not the pedagogy that must be fitted to the students but the students who must accept an untouchable method' (p. 292). Under these conditions, while teachers may 'seem to be in charge', and at a superficial level they are, at a more profound level it is students who 'actually control, manage, and shape the behavior of their teachers. Students reward teachers by complying. They punish by resisting' (p. 292). In these circumstances, what is occurring is that an 'authoritarian pedagogy' is shaping young people in ways that are not consistent with their true nature; their controlling behaviour can be changed, 'but they must be taught how' (p. 292). Two fundamental conditions have to be met for this change to occur:

> [First] the whole school faculty and school community – not the individual teacher – must be the unit of change; and [second] there must be patience and persistence of application, since students can be expected to resist changes to a system they can predict and know how to control. (p. 292)

The stakes are indeed incredibly high here, because what has implicitly been constructed and held in place by educational policy is an educational edifice that has to be dramatically turned around through a reversal of responsibility and control: 'The students' stake in maintaining the pedagogy of poverty is of the strongest possible kind: it absolves them of responsibility for learning and puts the burden on the teachers, who must be accountable for *making* them learn' (p.292). None of this need necessarily be so, because we know from the extensive experiences of accomplished teachers what good pedagogy looks like. In his typically provisional way, Haberman (1991) argues that 'good teaching' is likely to be occurring when students

- are involved with issues they regard as vital concerns . . .
- are involved with explanations of human differences . . .
- are being helped to see major concepts, big ideas, and general principles and are not merely engaged in the pursuit of isolated facts . . .
- are involved in planning what they will be doing . . .
- are involved with applying ideals such as fairness, equity, or justice to their world . . .
- are actively involved doing things rather than watching . . .
- are directly involved in a real-life experience . . .
- are actively involved in heterogeneous groups . . .

- are asked to think about an idea in a way that questions common sense or a widely accepted assumption, that relates new ideas to ones learned previously, or that applies an idea to the problems of living . . .
- are involved in redoing, polishing, or perfecting their work . . .
- have teachers who involve them with the technology of information access . . . and
- are involved in reflecting on their own lives and how they have come to believe and feel as they do. (pp. 293–4)

A way of drawing some of this complexity together is to say that the kind of leadership, school culture and organization necessary to turn around the dramatic circumstances confronting high schools in the United States and elsewhere, is to forcefully argue for a major shift of policy emphasis in the direction alluded to in the arguments presented here. I can best sum up that policy trajectory diagrammatically, and I will do so in Figure 3.1 without further elaboration.

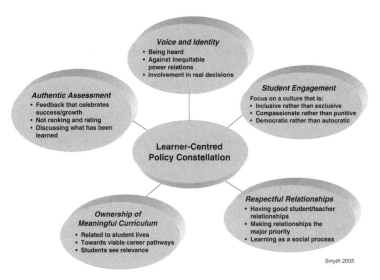

Figure 3.1 Learner-Centred Policy Constellation.

The evidence for this kind of policy redirection is powerful, incontrovertible and desperately overdue (Smyth et al., 2000). As Noddings (2005) has noted, there is nothing to be gained by persisting with policies, such as No Child Left Behind, that are based on 'threats', 'punishments' and 'pernicious comparisons'. The time is indeed right for a move away from structural and governance reforms, and towards relational reforms – ones that are centrally concerned with fostering confidence, trust and respect (Willie, 2000) and that have a commitment to dignity, humanity, belongingness and connectedness, while acknowledging the importance of rigour, relevance and relatedness (Smyth and McInerney, 2007a).

It is not that there is lack of understanding of the crucial importance of relationships, as I hope I have been able to demonstrate so far in this chapter and as is self-evident in some parts of the literature (Newmann, 1992; Comer, 1993; 2004; Meier, 1995; Newmann and Wehlage, 1995; Newmann and Associates, 1996). The issue is rather one of a deficit of political will and imagination to want to put 'relational ties around the interests of students' (Bryk and Schneider, 2002, p. 6) who are put in the centre of the educational frame. Comer (2004) argues that such an emphasis need not deny the importance of high standards, high expectations and accountability, but rather that it involves a shift in emphasis on the means for getting there. It would not be too fine a point to say that, at the moment, muscular and punitive approaches are undisputedly holding sway through dominant high stakes accountability approaches based on test scores. It is a case, Comer (2004) says, of 'right church, but wrong pew' (p. 2), and he puts the message simply, elegantly and stunningly in these terms:

> The direction to the right pew in education – like the real estate mantra of location, location, location – is relationships, relationships, relationships. Good relationships among and between the people in the institutions that influence the quality of child

life, largely home and school, make good child and adolescent rearing and development possible. (p. 2)

It all comes down to a case of needing to create 'a relationship context in all schools' (Comer, 2004, p. 2) – not just for a few privileged students but also for the estimated 15 million young people living in poverty in the United States. Whether schools are able to work this out or not has much to do with the degree to which young people are prepared to trust the institution of schooling by acknowledging and affirming the 'institutional legitimacy' of the school (Erickson, 1987, p. 341) – and surely that is the test with the highest stakes of all.

To illustrate how a school that was demonstrably 'failing' when it relied upon increasingly muscular and managerialist approaches, and how it brought on the soft revolution by working within 'the system' to subversively place the interests of young people first, I will turn to the case study of a school I have investigated and described. It really is a compelling story about how a school, its teachers and young people, found the internal resources with which to confront a failing school that was not meeting the needs of young people, and turning the school around by overcoming the impediments and making the school 'work for them'.

CLIMBING OVER THE ROCKS IN THE ROAD: THE CASE OF MANGO HIGH SCHOOL

There is a dilemma when it comes to reforming schools along the lines I am suggesting and in ways that improve learning – the problem is the growing mismatch within formal educational policy in terms of what is required, on the one hand, and what is likely to work at the school and classroom level, on the other. There is increasing evidence that schools are not meeting the needs of growing numbers of young people, especially those at the secondary level. The evidence is that significant numbers of young people are becoming disengaged from and 'dropping out' of school (see, e.g., Smyth et al., 2003; Orfield, 2004; Bridgeland et al., 2006). For those young people whose backgrounds have placed them at a 'disadvantage', the statistics are even more disturbing.

The official educational policy response to these trends has been an increase in approaches that emphasize accountability, increased reporting to parents, more testing, performance aimed at meeting standards and targets, greater parental choice of schools and, in general, a more prescriptive curriculum and more prescriptive modes of assessment (Fielding, 2001; Giroux and Schmidt, 2004; Codd, 2005; Smyth, 2005a; Gunter, 2006). For example, in the Australian context, the federal government's *Schools Assistance (Learning Together–Achievement through Choice and Opportunity) Act, 2004* made $33 billion of funding available to schools between 2005 and 2008, dependent upon schools and state governments satisfying certain demands: that schools report student performance on an A–E grading scale; that reports to parents be in 'plain English'; that students be ranked in comparison to their peers in each classroom; that student performance on a school-wide basis be made available publicly; that schools report publicly on staff attendance, retention and student attendance on a school-by-school basis; that schools meet detailed standards of performance and targets benchmarked against OECD (PISA) standards; that there be common national testing in reading, writing and numeracy; that every classroom display a statement of a 'national framework of values'; and that every school have a functioning flagpole displaying the Australian flag. The American context is similar to that in Australia, and the rest of the western world is following similar policy objectives. Raider-Roth (2005a) summarizes what amounts to a growing deficit of trust in schools in this way:

As a society, we no longer trust principals to make curricular decisions for their schools, as is evidenced by district-wide, city-wide, and statewide curricular initiatives such as teacher

guides, decisions to purchase uniform textbooks, and curriculum plans for all teachers. We no longer trust teachers to
make curricular and classroom decisions, as is evidenced by
the widespread implementation of standardized curricular.
The aggressive proliferation of standardized testing similarly
communicates our profound distrust of teachers' capacity to
teach. The message proclaimed by these tests is that teachers
do not know what children need to learn nor can they figure
out how to assess whether children are indeed learning. Finally
and most disturbingly, we are losing trust in children's drive to
learn, as is evidenced by the implementation of high stakes testing across the country, which suggests that unless children are
threatened with dire consequences of failing or not graduating,
they will not learn. (p. 17)

The problem with this policy agenda and the relay effects which
flow from it, is that it

has devastatingly eroded . . . [the] foundations of the teach-
ing-learning enterprise [and] teachers and researchers are
assiduously working to grasp, describe, resurrect, or otherwise
hold on to what we know sustains human capacity to construct
knowledge. (Raider-Roth, 2005a, pp. 17–18)

The Australian secondary I want to describe in a moment, that was
operating in difficult and complex circumstances, is illustrative of
what can occur when a school seriously looks at itself and embarks
on a process of reinventing itself by inserting 'relationships' into
all aspects of what it was doing. Later I will expand on how this
school, which I will call Mango High School, pursued the notion
of 'relational power' as part of a transformational pedagogy. What
was being attempted at the time of the study in 2004 was far from
complete, but the school felt that this approach was relevant for
its students, who were predominantly from working-class and

Aboriginal backgrounds in a remote part of Australia. Trying to coerce unmotivated and unwilling students to learn had been attempted previously and was found not to be a viable option in this school. The reference to 'rocks in the road' alludes to how a disadvantaged secondary school was trying to overcome the institutional impediments in the way of young people's learning.

The reinvigorated emphasis on relationships at Mango High was not a 'feel good' exercise; such an approach was unlikely to lead to any improvement in the life chances of these students. Rather, what was attempted was a process of inserting relationships into the processes of the school within a context of pursuing rigorous and productive learning.

The overarching agenda involved the teachers and school leadership seeking to navigate a pathway for these students around a different set of relationships and what happened when the students had 'relational power' (Mediratta, 2004; Warren, 2005, p. 136) over their learning.

The more general argument behind this case is that when schools experience problems with student disengagement, disaffection and alienation, what they are experiencing is a 'crisis of authority' (Sidorkin, 2002) in their relationships. The genesis of this breakdown in authority resides more generally in what Sidorkin (2002) argues to be a wider tendency over the past century in which schools have been 'steadily losing traditional means of control over students' (p. 53) and little creative thinking has occurred as to how to deal with this situation. While not endorsing a return to harsh authoritarian ways, Sidorkin (2002) argues that this crisis of authority is directly linked to the limits schools have over the 'power to expel and the power to inflict pain' (p. 54) upon students. In this situation, the nagging question that remains institutionally, and more specifically for schools, is: 'How do you run an organization where workers have very little incentive to work and their supervisors have very little power to force them?' (Sidorkin, 2002, p. 54). Herein lies the crux of the issue: how to understand and respond educationally to the issue of students' emotional, psychological and physical disengagement from school. Sidorkin (2002) puts it succinctly:

> A teacher's main challenge is to organize and direct an activity that dramatically lacks intrinsic motivation without the use of violence. No other social institution operates in this way. How do you make people do something they don't want to do? Writing warning slips, yelling, lunch detention, shaming, cajoling, begging, bribing, threatening, praising – all of these and many other tricks of the trade are notoriously unreliable. (p. 56)

The central question is how to be realistic about the limitations of what is possible for the schooling of young people while simultaneously acknowledging the inherently relational nature of young people. A study by the Australian Centre for Equity through Education and the Australian Youth Research Centre (2001) found that among young people 'at risk' of leaving school, 'the most important factors connecting young people to school were linked to relationships – friendship with other students and relationships with teachers that involved mutual respect and responsibility' (p. 7). These are sentiments increasingly being echoed in other countries as well, most notably in the United States, in research on what is being called the 'silent epidemic' (Bridgeland et al., 2006) and that precipitated a National State Governors' summit on the issue (National Governors Association, 2007). This raises the question of how might we think about and organize schools in a way that is consistent with young people's inherently relational nature. In this regard, current emphases on structural and behaviourally oriented reforms are proving to be misplaced in terms of their relevance and may be harmful and damaging to young people. As Sidorkin (2002) put it, 'The crisis of authority requires rethinking the institution of schooling in a way that provides some ground for adult authority to be re-established without reverting to traditional methods of exclusion and punishment' (p. 60). What needs to be pursued are ways of thinking and acting in schools that tackle this crisis of authority, and a way of doing this is to focus on how schools reinvent themselves around relationships – ones that go considerably beyond somewhat naïve child-centred pedagogies. In other words, there needs to be a fundamental reworking of schools so that they have a focus on a 'pedagogy of relations', which is to say, an approach that acknowledges

> that students will be attracted to school because of the quality of human relationships, the quality of communal experiences there. In other words, students will want to go to school not because of what they will do but because of who they will meet. (Sidorkin, 2002, p. 80)

At the moment, there is a trade-off of sorts being made by young people for compliance. Some young people are prepared to pay the price for boring, irrelevant and uninspiring schooling in order to have the social contact with one another that schools provide. The phenomenon of some young people persisting with schooling *despite* its perceived inadequacy, for largely social reasons of peer social contact, is well documented in places as diverse as the United States (Fine, 1991), England (Willis, 1977), Ireland (Fagan, 1995), Canada (Dei et al., 1997) and Australia (Smyth et al., 2004). However, as Comer (2004) points out, in the absence of compelling incentives such as social contact with peers, when schools persist in regarding 'academic learning as a mechanical process governed solely by genetically determined intelligence and individual will' (p. 3), this is no longer an effective approach. Contemporary students are not prepared to be treated as inanimate machines into which information is either poured or tacked on. Few 'will sit and take in what they often consider to be irrelevant information when there are so many exciting opportunities for learning outside of school' (Comer, 2004, pp. 3–4).

The driving priority here is clear: 'What we need to do now is restore the power of relations in schools' (Sidorkin, 2002, p. 80). The research question in the study of Mango High pursued this, namely: What does a school experiencing a 'crisis of authority' look like when it finds the internal resources to reinvent itself as a relational school? Furthermore, what does this mean for student learning and students' willingness to persist with school?

If the conditions necessary to successfully engage students in schools are ignored, then it could be argued that we are complicit in perpetuating educational policy failure. Following policies that do not work and that can damage schools, teachers and students raises profound moral and ethical questions.

THE WIDER CONTEXT OF MANGO HIGH SCHOOL AND ITS CONTEXT

Large numbers of students in the Northern Territory (NT) of Australia fall into one or more of the 'risk categories' reported in the educational literature of young adolescents who fail to complete secondary school education or who have a less than satisfying and rewarding experience of schooling. While there are a number of possible explanations for the debilitating and extenuating circumstances that contribute to low school completion rates in the Northern Territory, by far the most significant is the fact that 38% of the government school population is indigenous. Furthermore, the high percentage of the population living in remote areas brings additional challenges of diseconomies of scale, isolation and infrastructure difficulties (Productivity Commission Report, 2003).

The context of the Northern Territory itself is important here:

While the Northern Territory's 1, 346, 200 square kilometres occupy 17% of the Australian land mass, its 198, 000 inhabitants represent only one per cent of the country's population

(ABS, 2003a). Just under 12, 000 of these inhabitants are [of] secondary [school] age. (Northern Territory Government, 2004, p. 16)

With transience of approximately 10% of the population moving into or out of the Territory each year, this means that 'young people come into Territory schools from all over Australia in much higher proportions than occurs in other states . . . A high level of intra-territory transience parallels this external transience as well' (p. 17). Added to this, 'Approximately 31% of Territorians speak a language other than English at home. Of these, half speak Australian Indigenous languages' (p. 17).

At the time of the study, school completion rates (defined as 'students who obtain a year 12 certificate as a percentage of the potential year 12 population' (16-year-olds) [Productivity Commission, 2003]) in the Northern Territory compare unfavourably with the rest of Australia. According to the Productivity Commission's (2003) 'Report on Government Services', estimated school completion rates in urban areas of the Northern Territory were 43% (35% for male students, 50% for female students) compared to national figures of 69% (64% for male and 74% for female students) (Table 3.9, p. 3.35 and Table 3.10, p. 3.36). Not much has changed in the intervening period, and if anything they have worsened as a result of economic conditions.

These conditions make the Northern Territory one of the most complex and challenging educational environments in Australia, and an important one to try to understand.

Mango High School, the case study school, was self-selected for this research by responding to a call for expressions of interest. We asked for participation from a high school with a population of students usually referred to as 'at risk' of school failure, but that also felt it was working successfully to retain its students. Mango High School is located in a suburban community and has an enrolment of approximately 800 students and 70 teachers.

The school has been in existence for about 20 years and caters to children from years 8 to 12 (12–16 years old). A newly created middle-school programme (in years 8 and 9 [aged 12–13 years]) supports student transition from primary to secondary school. The programme includes a strong pastoral care component, a reduced need for students to move from teacher to teacher throughout the day and curriculum integration between some subject areas. An accelerated programme, known as Advanced Learning for High Achievers (ALFHA), provides for students in years 8–10 (12–14 years old) with high academic potential in four core subjects. The *Futures Beacon, 'No Dole'* programme introduced in the school in 2003 involves students signing a pledge that commits them to finding a job or going on to further education after year 10. At the time of the study, Mango High School was trying to reinvent itself and counteract a history of behavioural problems, violence, drugs, a lack of hope among students and staff, and unfavourable reporting in the press.

THE RESEARCH PROBLEM AND METHODOLOGY

The labelling of students as 'at risk' is an individualistic approach that locates the source of failure within the students themselves, their families, their teachers or their schools. However, it is possible to reframe this problem by reconfiguring the phenomenon of 'at risk' students and their schooling as a socially constructed condition which is capable of analysis at a number of levels using fresh perspectives (see Smyth, 2005b). What is of particular interest in relation to these kind of students is the socially constructed conditions that enabled students who might otherwise have 'dropped out' to stay engaged in schooling.

We were therefore interested in students who stayed in school 'against the odds'. What are the conditions that occur in such a school and its community that amount to new ways of understanding and addressing the barriers to school engagement? How can a school reconfigure and reinterpret itself to ensure that students do not become 'exiles'? We wanted to undertake a study that was concerned with focusing on 'hope' rather than 'despair' (Stanton-Salazar, 2001). We aimed to find out more about how these processes occurred by studying them closely in one school.

The overall strategy employed in trying to understand this question was one of 'voiced research' (Smyth, 1999), in which we accessed 'voices from inside the school' (Poplin and Weeres, 1992). We conducted

- embedded' interviews (Pollard et al., 1994) with 14 teachers (including the principal, two assistants and the school counsellor)
- classroom observations of 8 teachers (from those interviewed) including: year 9 English, year 10 English, year 8 Special Education class × 2, year 9 Science, year 8 Social Science, year 8 Maths, and year 9 Maths
- 4 student focus group discussions with years 9, 10, 11 and 12 with an average of 6–8 students (i.e. approximately 30 students).

We progressively 'thematized' the transcripts in a process of 'dialectical theory-building' (Lather, 1986; Smyth, 1998) to clarify and reconstruct existing theory, in which generative themes that emerged from continuous and close reading of the data were checked for consistency in light of existing theory, and in turn 'counter interpretations' (Lather, 1986, p. 267) uncovered where these did not fit with extant theory.

NAVIGATING A PATHWAY TOWARDS RELATIONSHIPS

The metaphor of 'navigating a pathway' is a helpful one with which to explore and understand what occurred when Mango

confronted its 'crisis of authority' in 2003. As the media coverage
at the time and our subsequent interviews revealed, there was a
pressing need for the restoration of order and some ground rules
that everyone in the school agreed to, but equally important, there
was the need to create a collective sense that everyone, students
as well as teachers, were working together to move students along
a path to some valued and agreed upon end. It is important to
make the point that there was no formula or single universal way
of doing that, but what the school recognized was that the process
of reclamation had to be grounded in some major educational
ideas, which will be dealt with shortly. Having some degree of
consistency of purpose did not mean that everyone in the school
had to be in universal agreement. What it did mean was that for
the school to move forward in reinventing itself, there had to be a
broad consensus.

The starting point was one of optimism, hope and possibility,
rather than despair, deficits and punishment. Unless the school
was able to construct an image of itself and its students, parents
and staff that was worthwhile, then a spiralling culture of worth-
lessness and hopelessness would be likely to persist.

Crucial to this notion of a sense of worth was placing relationships at the centre of everything Mango High School did. How
people treated one another was regarded as crucial. It was not hard
to find evidence of how this was occurring from the viewpoint of
teachers as well as students. One of the ways it was most consistently presented to us was in terms of 'respect', reflected in people
regarding one another as worthwhile individuals, their backgrounds, aspirations, *where they are coming from*' (Teacher #11)
and where they are heading.

A central theme of relationships building within the school
concerned teachers being *realistic about the difficulties*' (Teacher
#7) in confronting these students and acknowledging the *chal-
lenging nature of these kids*' (Teacher #7). As one veteran teacher
framed it,

*We have a down-to-earth style and environment here. The whole
staff realizes that we have things to work on . . . The school isn't
beating around the bush on the difficulties we have, but we are
doing the best we can.* (Teacher #11)

Providing opportunities for students to get to know their
teachers and '*to see the human side of their teachers*' (Assistant
Principal), seemed to be paramount. As one teacher put it,
you need to get to '*know the kids and their homes . . . get to
know them socially*' (Teacher #3), and as another said, '*get to
know the kids and their parents*' (Teacher #4). Another emphasized '*understanding the cultural issues they bring with them*'
(Teacher #7).

Especially important in this school '*you need to get on with
them* [students]' (Teacher #10), and to do that '*you need to like
them*' (Teacher #11). As one assistant principal put it, '*these kids
learn the teachers first, then the subjects . . . these kids can spot
teachers who go through the motions*' and they '*switch off teachers
they don't like*'.

This mutual getting to know and understand one another, for
both teachers and students, was made possible by the fact that
'*there is a directness and honesty about these kids*' (Teacher #7).
Notwithstanding this, '*it takes time to build up a picture of these
kids*' (Teacher #4), and continually conveying the message to students '*that you care*' (Teacher #1) seemed to be part of a broader
strategy, as one teacher put it, of '*trying to make them strong and
powerful people*' (Teacher #3).

Part of knowing students was '*earning their respect*' (Teacher #6),
which was considered crucial to ensuring educational success.
As one teacher said, '*these kids need continuity with teachers*'
(Teacher #8) and '*they will stay* [at school] *if they see a purpose*'
(Teacher #7); indeed their '*success depends on their seeing a purpose*' (Teacher #7). A teacher of twenty-five years' experience,
fourteen of them at Mango, put it this way:

Mainstream classes have a limited attention span. Activities have to be highly structured. You tend to give them things that are more structured, and only talk for about 5 minutes. They respond to things like competitions, and things that have rewards. They are big on fairness and they call a spade a spade . . . Most teachers at this school persevere with these students. If you are prepared to talk with them one-on-one then you can sometimes make a difference . . . They will only open up to you . . . and you will only get to the issues in the one-to-one conversations. (Teacher #11)

He spoke of the preparedness of his colleagues to '*go the extra mile*' in terms of the '*willingness of many teachers to go beyond the call of duty. The reason we do this is for the benefit of the students in the long haul. It is a touchy issue at times because they are overworked.*' Mango had a strong emphasis

> on processes for chasing kids down the line (Teacher #5), *of not letting things go . . . the teachers here follow through on things a great deal – on behaviour and how students are going –* [mentioned a particular student]. *He has got a diary going, spoken to his dad. In a couple of months he will be on track. It's just a case of not letting him go. It would be easy to do that.* (Teacher #8)

In open acknowledgement of the need to enrich the learning landscape of these students, there was much talk about '*continually providing them* [students] *with opportunities*' (Principal), of students having opportunities they '*might not otherwise have*', and using every opportunity to bring in '*outsiders to give kids pathways*' (Assistant Principal).

While behaviour management existed at a policy level in the school, it seemed to reside much more at a practical classroom level in having sound working relationships with students, '*making rules explicit so students have choices*' [and of] '*getting students to see and explain [and work through] the consequences of their actions*' (Teacher #7). There was a school-wide emphasis on '*continually modelling good performance*' (Principal) in all kinds of ways, an '*emphasis on courtesy and respect*' (Assistant Principal), on '*setting boundaries*' for behaviour, being '*firm but fair*' (Teacher #11), '*following up little things before they get big*' (Assistant Principal), and '*not letting things go*' (Teacher #8), with lots of '*follow through*' (Teacher #4). Equally, not having an authoritarian approach to discipline seemed to go hand-in-hand with '*using humour*' (Teacher #5) and a '*belief in the need to have fun*' (Assistant Principal). In an illustration of how the school had converted behaviour management into everyone's issue, the acting principal responded as follows when asked about the existence of a 'time-out', 'withdrawal' or 'focus room' for miscreants:

> *We don't have a time-out room – withdrawal room – went through several processes – I was not comfortable with it and I felt that people were using it as a cop-out – it was for someone disrupting the learning process – but there had to be some follow up by the teacher – and some kids like to go to withdrawal room – the person in charge of the withdrawal room process didn't do anything – so we left it and we have worked without it . . . the teachers have abandoned this themselves unconsciously – they didn't like coming here and supervising naughty kids – another side of it was that some students were missing a lot of class, missing a lot of learning . . . it died a natural death – died of malnutrition – a couple of individuals said 'where is the withdrawal room?' Well, we haven't got one at the moment and that's all that's been said.*

There were other things the school had embarked upon that helped to turn the situation around, including teachers placing much greater emphasis on pastoral care in keeping track of students who were having difficulties and contacting families before problems escalated – this was supported by the school appointing a full-time attendance officer; school violence was markedly reduced by involving local police in regular attendance at the school, working on positive activities with students; mentoring support was provided by senior teachers to younger teachers so that classroom problems were able to be detected much earlier than previously; extended, continuing conversations were occurring across the whole school focused on ensuring that students were engaged and succeeding at school; and a general atmosphere had been created within the school in which the school leaders 'talked up' the positive achievements of the school and the students in ways that enhanced identity and self-esteem – something that had been absent in earlier times when the school received only negative publicity. But probably one of the most significant changes was in the process of actively bringing the community into the school as part of a careers pathway programme to provide students with a clear focus in terms of where they saw themselves heading with their schooling.

Whether there were differences in pedagogical style or substance in how teachers went about their classroom teaching seemed to be less important than the fact that teachers in this school appeared to be prepared to emphasize some bigger issues, such as the importance of relationships as a basis for changing the culture of the school in ways that made it more amenable as a place of learning for these particular disadvantaged students.

WHEN STUDENTS HAVE 'RELATIONAL POWER': THE SCHOOL AS A SITE FOR IDENTITY FORMATION

The other side to what the school and the teachers were doing can be seen through students' views and their perceptions of increased agency over their learning. At the centre of our discussion here is the concept of 'relational power' (Warren, 2005), a notion that draws its theoretical sustenance from the closely related notion of social capital (Coleman, 1988; Bourdieu, 1997). This is part of a wider paradigmatic shift underway in school reform (Romano, 2000; Bryk and Schneider, 2002; Romano and Glasnock, 2002; Sidorkin, 2002; Bingham and Sidorkin, 2004; Raider-Roth, 2005a) that is beginning to acknowledge the primary importance of relationships within structural grass-roots school reform (Smyth, 2004; Smyth and McInerney, 2007b).

Relational power, while generally used to refer to the way in which collaboration and trust is created across and among constituent groups in schools and their communities, also has considerable currency when used to refer to resources or capacities for redressing inequalities in schooling, most notably in terms of who is provided with the resources necessary to succeed at school. In other words, relational power refers to the 'set of resources that inhere in relationships of trust and cooperation between and among people' (Warren, 2005, p. 136). It can be a potent resource for 'transforming the internal capacity of schools' (Medirratta, 2004, p. 16), as was evident at Mango High School. In advancing this, Bryk and Schneider (2002) have developed what they refer to as a 'grounded theory of relational trust' (p. 124). They describe 'relational trust' as a key resource in school improvement which has core elements of 'respect', 'personal regard', 'competence' and 'integrity' (p. 124) at all levels of the school, including in and across social exchanges between teachers, principals, students, parents and ancillary staff.

The point here is that when relationships among students, teachers, parents and the community are damaged, corrupted, corroded or are not established, then students suffer. As Warren (2005) put it, 'Relational power [emphasizes] the "power to" get things done collectively' (p. 138) and it is based on 'the need to confront power inequalities' (p. 138). One of the most significant power inequalities in schools is the lack of opportunity for students to have a say in their learning.

Students may indeed have more relational power than we give them credit for when it comes to their acceptance or rejection of the conditions under which they learn. I want to build upon and extend Raider-Roth's (2005b) notion that 'students read the relational tenor of their classroom' (p. 588), and their learning may be heavily dependent on their willingness and 'capacity to trust their knowledge' (p. 588). In other words, what students are willing to 'share', as well as 'suppress', in terms of revelations central to their learning, may not be 'a reflection of their full body of knowledge, but rather that which they think is deemed "fit" to bring to school' (p. 588). How, and in what ways, students trust their teachers and the culture of the school 'intersects with the kind of internal trust that students must construct in order to learn effectively' (p. 588).

Invoking Gilligan (1982), Noblit (1993) argues that in these situations there is an instance of 'caring [that] is context dependent and reciprocal' (p. 35). In other words, teachers are continually involved in 'reciprocal negotiation' (Noblit, 1993, p. 37): '[A] willingness [of the teacher] to take responsibility for children to participate in [their learning], and from children themselves who, after all can and often do deny adults the right to control them' (p. 37). Socially constructed and legitimated construals like this shift us in the direction of an 'emphasis on collectivity' (Noblit, 1993, p. 37). Such thinking moves us beyond simplistic dualisms of 'teacher-centered' and 'student-centered' approaches by arguing that 'a caring relationship [is not] an equal relationship' (p. 26), which is to say, 'caring in classrooms is not about democracy – it is about the ethical use of power' (p. 24) and student attachment.

At Mango High, students had much to say about the importance of relationships to their learning and the relational conditions that made learning possible for them. By way of a caveat, these students were talking to us as 'strange' adults, and their answers may thus appear to be less expansive than might otherwise have been the case with adults they knew better.

In responding to the question of what they liked most about school, students at Mango High predictably emphasized the social aspect, but it was more complex than that: *'The good thing about school is seeing your friends. We don't see school as cool, we just don't have a choice but we want to do it. If we had a choice we would still come here'* (Year 9 students). Once students had made their point about the importance of sociability to their identity formation at school, other more complex explanations emerged:

> *We want to get an education. Some people don't appreciate what the teachers are trying to do for us. Teachers are just human beings and are just like us. The school is putting us on a pathway – getting social skills – being around people every day – you have to do little oral presentations in class.* (Year 12 students)

While in some students' minds there was clearly utility to schooling, there was still some puzzlement among others as to exactly how some aspects of school fit together for them. For example: *'School helps us to make choices – I think the electives are the classes that you can see will be useful – computers and home eco. Maths can be an important subject – but what the hell is this stuff?'* [meaning mathematics] (Year 9 students). Understandably, ambiguity was never far away for some students: *'It's a good school – there's heaps stuff wrong with it but basically it's a good school. It's a major part of your life – it's been there every day since you were little'* (Year 12 students). It is important to emphasize (in addition to what has already been mentioned) the changes that were being made to try to turn the school around – for example, smaller classes. At Mango, this was crucial to providing students with the opportunity to get to know their teachers, and through that, to deepen relationships regarded as fundamental to their learning:

Classes are smaller here and there is more one-on-one with the teachers – it's good to have a smaller class – you get to discuss things with the teacher. We're not up there with [two nearby schools] but we still get a really good education – if you are willing to put in the effort – it's the same curriculum – it's the same standard, if you are willing to work. (Year 12 student)

Some students described positive pedagogical relationships that were invariably linked with teachers respecting them as learners:

Teachers treat us as equals; good atmosphere; teachers respect you. (Year 12 students)

I like teachers that get their point around [sic]; teachers who let you talk; I don't like a quiet class. I enjoy coming to school – like learning – hate class clowns and attention seeking people. Teachers who know how to handle kids; not so strict here as other schools – it's more laid back – the kids can do their things at their own pace; we feel comfortable and want to come to school. (Year 10 Students)

Forming a learning identity was, therefore, viewed in terms of how students saw teachers as creating the relational conditions for attachment, belongingness, and sense of community, and teachers' capacity to focus on what was important. In responding to questions about what it was like being a student in this school and what they liked most about the school, some year 11 students made the following comments:

[It's a] smaller school; more attention from teachers; you become attached; everyone knows each other here; teachers who are flexible; teachers who are easy to speak to; we like being actively involved; where teachers know each other; teachers who communicate; teachers are concerned about your future and if you are motivated they will try and help you; we don't have to wear a

95

uniform – it's self-expression – it's really good – it's a superficial thing; you have to be comfortable with what you are wearing – it helps you learn if you are comfortable.

What we can see being enacted here are the ways in which some students, at least, are negotiating relational learning identities for themselves within the school. They spoke of teachers as constituting the human face of schools and the kind of relationships that followed from that. An illustration of this is what students labelled as aspects of 'good' teaching, which they saw as inseparable from what they described as the 'good teacher':

> *able to relate to the student; willing to accept questions and not to just brush over it; it's got to [be able to] relate; fairly pleasant and understanding; respect and just smiling [sic] and stuff, and if you have the relationship no matter what the problem is, you can go to them anytime.* (Year 11 students)

What the students are alluding to in these comments is the overall process of the school humanizing itself, from a place that was fairly out of control, wracked by violence, that had a poor public image, and that was not at all conducive to student learning. The turning point was the realization by the school that the confrontational way of doing things was not working for these disadvantaged students and that what was required was a different approach that put the interests of students and their learning first.

The overlap between 'learning' and having 'fun' was consistently commented on: '*Our physics teacher is really good and we have fun in the class but we learn a lot and we really enjoy it*' (Year 11 student). In response to the question of how the school and its teachers were helping them along valued learning pathways to a future, some year 9 students put it like this:

> *It's better when they give you work – allow you to have fun and work at the same time – teachers who know their stuff.*

When she is not doing all the talking and everyone gets to say something.

It's hard to absorb information if you don't enjoy what she's talking about – you just tune off.

Enjoying a subject – it's got to be interesting – it's got to be two sided – bringing your views, when the teacher listens to what your views are on something and you get to have a say.

Some students talked about the importance of knowing their teachers as people, and often out-of-school opportunities facilitated this: '*the students here don't feel they need to be confined [sic]– they can be themselves – relaxed; [lots of giggles] socialize with the teachers a lot more*' (Year 11 student). Part of this apparent family feeling seemed to be due to the way some students had experienced continuity in their relationships with one another and their teachers:

it's got a good atmosphere and the teachers really help and most of us have been here since year 8 and the teachers are here for us. (Year 11 student)

I went away for 4 months and mum said if I wanted to go to XXXX College I could. I said I wanted to come back here because I knew all the teachers and everything, and to go somewhere else I'd have to start all over again. (Year 11 student)

All of us have been here since year 8 – and we are now on a friendship basis with them more so than as teachers – you want to learn because the teachers here are putting in to help you. (Year 12 student)

According to other students, teachers who understood and acknowledged the complexity of young lives accommodated what students were saying in their teaching:

Life is complicated – I have work outside – have to learn how to manage time – social life, school life and work life. (Year 10 student)

97

Teachers help you plan your time – in home room they have a time management thing and you make out a list with the help of the teacher. (Year 10 student)

As one year 9 student put it, 'We can get lots of help from the teachers without getting behind in stuff – the teachers care and we have been to schools where teachers don't care' (Year 9 student). Another student summed up the essence of relationships with teachers in the school in this way: 'they give a damn about what we are doing' (Year 12 student). Lest we give the impression here that Mango was some kind of idealistic student nirvana, when asked about how much say they were given over their learning, two students extinguished any delusions:

not much – they ask you what you want to learn but we still do what they want us to learn. (Year 9 student)

[Say in what you learn?] – no we don't have any say . . . it's like you're doing this . . . in classrooms we don't get a say . . . hardly ever go out to the community – most of the stuff is in the classroom. (Year 10 student)

Students labelled as respectful teachers who knew their subject matter, were open to student suggestions, made students feel 'important' and offered encouragement:

A good maths teacher is one who explains things – someone who doesn't need to go and look in a book, and it shows that the teacher knows what they are doing.

Getting the class involved – if the teacher doesn't know the answer and someone in the class might know.

The best teachers are the ones that are involved with you and try and get to know you and are involved with the students – it makes you feel important. (Year 10 students)

[What do they do?] have good hand movements – being confident when they are talking then we feel that they know what they are talking about – confident in themselves so kids don't run all over them. (Year 10 student)

You need to know if you are capable of doing it –– they encourage you to do it – both in class and out of class – if your work piles up they let you have till Friday, and you think, 'I can do this'. (Year 10 student)

We act like we get treated – respect – we do respect our elders but if they don't respect us we don't respect them – they have to earn our respect . . . people who carry grudges don't get our respect. (Year 10 students)

Teachers who go the extra mile – they are prepared to stay the extra time. (Year 10 student)

It is noteworthy to comment here on the broadly favourable responses of students to their school. It is well established in the educational literature that students are very perceptive witnesses on what helps or hinders their learning. Students from challenging backgrounds, like the ones in this case-study school, also have a way of being disarmingly honest, and as educators we need to be more attuned to their views. However, it is certainly not the case that all students presented the same views, as the above instances of student reservations about school attest: 'We don't see school as cool, we just don't have a choice'; 'What the hell is this stuff [mathematics]?'; 'there's heaps stuff wrong'; 'we still do what they [the teachers] want us to do'; and 'in classrooms we don't get a say'. What the student comments reflect is something of a balanced affirmation that they found the changes underway in the school to be ones that broadly assisted them in their learning, notwithstanding some unresolved difficulties with the nature of schooling itself.

LEADERSHIP MATTERS!

In many respects, the story being told here was a fairly remarkable one (although not entirely unique – see May, 1994; Vibert et al. with Forrest and Will, 2001; Vibert et al., 2002; Smyth and McInerney, 2007a) of a school that had gone through a significant set of changes (highlighted earlier), and how this occurred deserves some words of explanation. At one level, the account can be read as if there was total unanimity among all informants we spoke to in the school (students, teachers and school leaders). There is an element of truth in that. However, although informants felt that the school had turned an important corner, they were quick to acknowledge that there was still a great deal of ground to be covered in terms of improvement. Participants emphasized that what they had achieved so far was still very provisional and tentative. It is important to note this because of the seemingly uniform, positive tone in many of the comments. It is also important to note the crucial part that the school leadership clearly played in the reform processes that were underway.

There were a number of aspects of the school leadership that highlight how the conditions conducive to change were fostered in the school, most notably in two broad ways. First, getting the school and its community to acknowledge that the existing situation was 'out of control', that it was no longer tenable and had to be directly confronted. For example, the high levels of violence, the amount of swearing and bad language, the high levels of student absenteeism, the low levels of students completing school, the large number of students suspended from school, gangs and violence, and generally alienated, disaffected and disengaged students. The untenable nature of the existing situation was not difficult to establish, particularly given the negative media portrayal of the school in the previous few years and the school's own behavioural records. For example, during the school term prior to the interviews taking place, there had been 47 school suspensions, the majority being boys in years 8 and 9 (12–13 years old). At the time of the interviews, three weeks into term, there had been no year 9 suspensions, which the assistant principal described as: pretty good for 180 kids. A year 10 girl had been suspended for 5 days for using offensive language to a teacher, and a year 11 boy for 10 days for continually swearing in a public place. Changes of the kind occurring in the school can to some degree be attributed to the school reinventing itself around the idea that without the relational work (Smyth, 2007; Smyth et al., 2010) necessary to establish the boundaries for respect, learning for many of the students would be almost impossible. It was hard to say how enduring these changes might be, but without them it was hard to see an optimistic future.

Second, once members of the school community were able to openly acknowledge that the school had been 'failing', there was a growing preparedness to look at alternatives. The interview data reflect some basic principles that were being strenuously promoted within the school, including the following:

Relationships and Welfare of Students

- Courteous and respectful relationships were regarded as being crucial.
- The welfare of students had to prevail as being central to any reform.
- There had to be processes in place in the school to ensure that no student 'fell through the cracks' in the sense that contact was maintained with all students and their families, regardless.
- Relationships with 'difficult' students were seen as having to begin in out-of-class activities, such as sporting activities, or during out-of-class excursions, during which students could get to see the human side of their teachers.

Establishing Boundaries for Learning

- Unacceptable behaviour was not to be tolerated.
- There had to be firm guidelines as to what constituted acceptable behaviour.

Focus and Organization around Learning

- Rigorous learning had to occur.
- In whatever it did, the school had to remain comprehensive in that students needed to be accepted into the school and to be given the opportunity to learn regardless of their background.
- Teachers involved in the reform process (a year 8 and 9 initiative) were to be provided with time release from teaching to plan and work together.
- Behaviour management problems (except for bad language) were not to be exclusively presented in terms of naughty or recalcitrant students, but rather as reflecting the need to present interesting, enjoyable and engaging learning activities for students; in other words, it was considered to be a curriculum issue.
- It was an aspect of the work of all leaders in the school to praise teachers and students for their successes.

Communication with Parents and the Community

- Every opportunity had to be taken to continually 'talk up' the successes of teachers, students and the school so that a consistent positive image of the school could be presented to the wider community.
- Part of the role of all teachers and leaders in the school was to communicate with parents in terms of what the school was trying to do.

- While being realistic about the magnitude of the difficulties being confronted by the school,[1] the wider community had to be kept informed about progress being made by the school in a way that made them feel proud the school was part of their community.

School reform is neither an easy nor straightforward task, as this example illustrates. Despite its negative history and reputation, Mango High School seems to have created the conditions necessary for its young people to construct viable identities for themselves as students and as people who can belong to the school community. Yet this is still an ambiguous and constantly evolving 'work in progress' with no formulas, universal procedures or easy fixes. What seems to have been of pivotal importance was the ability of the school community to recognize as insufficient the punitive approaches of the past and to choose instead to assert adult authority through the development of respectful relations which afforded students the relational power that they require to persist with schooling, against the odds.

The evidence presented here, while not itself establishing conclusive 'cause and effect' connections between respectful treatment of young people and enhanced learning, does nevertheless point to an obvious, indispensable and crucial, but difficult to establish, precursor to the conditions necessary for disadvantaged youngsters connecting to, belonging and remaining in school. Without that it seems that the most unfortunate aspects of the circuit of irrelevance of schooling, alienation and hopelessness cannot be interrupted.

NOTE

1 An indicator that the community perceptions of the school had begun to change and that things were different can be gauged by

the enrolment figures (in a context of parental school choice). In 2007, enrolments had grown to 750, up significantly from the 400 students in the year before the study. Furthermore, to quote from the principal, in 2007 there were 'more students in senior years than ever before [in the 21 year history of the school]' (Newsletter No. 1, March 2007).

CHAPTER 4

Critically Engaged 'Community Capacity Building' That 'Speaks Back' to Social Exclusion

INTRODUCTION

Looking for a place from which to start discussing the notion of 'community', which is the third aspect of this book, can be a confusing, bewildering and daunting task, even when coming at it from a vantage point that seeks to problematize it. I was, therefore, somewhat heartened by Jeremy Brent's (2009)[1] comment that it is a 'ubiquitous term' (p. 4) that deeply 'infiltrates much everyday thought and action' (p. 21) and is bandied about in local and national politics as well as in academic circles. Brent says that approaching it has to come with 'a health warning: handle with care' (p. 21). Exploring a complex idea like community does not lend itself at all well to 'cut and dried definitions' (p. 5). As Richard Johnson (2009) puts it in the introduction to Brent's book *Searching for Community*, exploring the notion of what community means involves a 'mapping not just [of] spaces or places, but also relevant arguments and ideas' (p. 4).

While much romanticized, and far too often not problematized in terms of 'how far a particular community practice opens up or closes down [possibilities] – and for whom', Johnson (2009) summarizes the essence of Brent's 'constructed' view of community as follows:

> Community isn't something that is given or can be relied on. Rather, the idea of community is attached to different forms of collective identity that have actually to be created. Community in this sense is always fragile and fractured, always takes variable forms and always involves particular kinds of power. It includes, embraces and empowers, but it also excludes. (p. 5)

This is a view of community that is far from settled – it is dynamic and evolving. This view of community is concerned with contesting and redefining how power works. As Brent (2009) put it in terms of his own experiences of community activity, 'Community activities are messy and conflictual, the opposite of . . . stasis and pacification', and to that extent community activities are invariably entered into by people who find ways into 'the maelstrom rather than succumb to it' (p. 212). In other words, when we speak about community we are entering the realm of collective actions that are connected to wider global flows of ideas, arguments and movements. Far from being a 'unitary or harmonious form' (Brent, 2009, p. 203), the notion of what a community is shifts around depending upon the issue, what is being struggled over and whose interests are at stake. Understandably, the use of such a confusing, contradictory and omnibus category for something so 'malleable and pliant' causes us to seriously consider whether we should be 'jettisoning it's use completely' (p. 204) – something that is unlikely to occur, for the very reason that it can be conveniently used to make it appear as if we all know and agree upon its meaning – which is a good way, in the end, to appear to have consensus.

WORKING FROM THE MARGINS – OR THE 'SPACES OF RADICAL OPENNESS'

Thinking in these ways brings me to the kind of reworking envisaged by black feminist bell hooks (1990) in her essay 'Choosing the margin as a space of radical openness'. As she puts it, for people whose lives have been diminished and impoverished, their ability to live 'depends on [their] ability to conceptualize alternatives' (hooks, 1990, p. 149). In a sense, it is their having been pushed to the margins by social and political forces that provides them with the 'space of radical openness [as] a margin – a profound edge' (p. 149) from which to construct alternative 'counter-hegemonic' cultural practices. hooks (1990) is at pains to make the point that marginality is 'much more than a site of deprivation . . . [rather] just the opposite . . . [a] site of radical possibility, a space of resistance' (p. 149). For her, 'spaces can tell stories and unfold histories' (hooks, 1990, p. 152). It is when marginality is chosen as a 'site of resistance' as distinct from being 'imposed' by 'oppressive structures' (p. 153), that 'we move in solidarity to erase the category colonized/colonizer' (p. 152). She invokes lines from singer Bob Marley: 'We refuse to be what you want us to be, we are what we are, and that's the way it's going to be' (p. 150). In other words, it is from this 'space of refusal' (p. 150) that alternatives are constructed – which is a most apposite place for me to begin to make the case for the voices of communities that have been silenced and 'done to'. If this has a slightly subversive or insurgent sound to it, then that is probably because it is.

As Corbett (2009) put it, drawing on Michel de Certeau's (1984) seminal book *The Practice of Everyday Life*, what we need is a 'frame for understanding how people who [are] supposed to be erased have managed to hang on' (p. 3). Extracting its essence, Corbett (2009a) summarizes de Certeau's idea as seeing 'social life as a continual dance between strategic power instituted and promoted in strategic institutional discourse and the on-the-ground tactical responses of those who are the objects of this power' (p. 2). Such place-specific constructions of identity and the sets of resistances and accommodations that come with them, are really an acknowledgement that 'power is negotiated and . . . institutional authority is always playing catch-up with resistance.

107

It is in a sense resistance that leads the dance of power rather than strategy' (Corbett, 2009b). This reversal of the conventional view of the hierarchical and institutional workings of power places the ball much more in the quarter of those who have traditionally been constructed as being 'powerless' and oppressed and positions them in a much more optimistic way as having agency in all kinds of ways, as I will go on to discuss shortly.

In a recent monograph entitled *What to Look for in Genuine Community Engagement*, my colleagues and I (Smyth et al., 2011) have argued that when the words community or urban renewal, community regeneration or neighbourhood renewal are used, it is invariably directed at communities that are deemed to be in need of being 'fixed up'. At one level, there is a considerable element of truth to this. These are seen as communities that often have a long history of 'problems' – poverty, family breakdown, unemployment, homelessness, mental health, substance abuse, domestic dysfunction or whatever other difficulties result in people being outside of the mainstream of society and at the fringes or the margins. The focus is, therefore, on: so-called 'risk factors' by; narrowing the gap; targeting resources; acknowledging past difficulties of a lack of a co-ordination; pursuing whole of-government joined-up responses; bringing residents and governments together; and, empowering residents in these communities in ways that they become part of the solution through being involved in decision making.

When notions of renewal are invoked it is invariably in association with communities that are deemed to be 'disadvantaged' or to be defective in some respects. The term 'disadvantaged' is in parentheses, indicating the need to challenge the conventional thinking that lies behind it and that usually accompanies the term. 'Disadvantage', as it is generally used, is a category that points the finger of blame, personalizes people in these communities as somehow being responsible for the circumstances in which they find themselves, and, in effect, insinuates that it is somehow their fault. An emphasis on fixing, refurbishing and restoring according to some largely invisible middle-class standard of the way lives ought to be led creates a considerable difficulty. No amount of consultation is going to conceal the fact that judgements are being made about the fundamental dysfunctional nature of such communities.

Explanations and portrayals of how people are made (or are even born that way), and their circumstances made to appear somehow accidental, unfortunate, almost natural and unavoidable – has considerable appeal to it at a certain level. We can see how the popular media in which we are soaked convey the message that such people have somehow made 'bad choices' and that they need remediation.

The way explanations are constructed does not make them necessarily correct, nor does it mean that there are not other equally valid and credible explanations as to how some people become 'disadvantaged' while others appear to be naturally 'advantaged'. The point is that explanations of occurrences like 'disadvantage' cannot be left residing at the level of the accidental – the truth is that 'disadvantage' is constructed, and as citizens we are all implicated to some extent in making it that way and in allowing it to continue that way.

Approaching the analysis of what is going on in this way might appear to mitigate the need for collective responsibility for the plight of the less fortunate and position blame at the level of the individuals concerned, but that is not a sound basis upon which to fundamentally alter or change the circumstances producing the inequalities in the first place.

It is not a large step, either, from notions of renewal to those of engagement. Community engagement is one of those apparently commonsense, plausible ideas that no one in their right mind could possibly be opposed to. It is such a compelling idea: that those who are excluded from the mainstream of society should be restored and made a prosperous part of it by being given a kind of relational makeover. What we need to do, so the thinking goes, is find ways of getting people who have fallen off the track back on it, into productive and rewarding (i.e. working) lives. What is supposedly needed is to give poor people help in undergoing this makeover. The broken communicative and other aspects of their lives that have become fractured and fragmented have to be repaired and those who are deemed to be 'disadvantaged' have to be provided with better alternative models to choose from. Along the way, they have to be better isolated and 'targeted' in terms of the identification of 'risk factors' so that the unfortunate 'cycles of disadvantage' they have become caught up in can be interrupted.

If only it were only so simple – and all that was required was a laminating over – then these problems would have been solved long ago, and we would not be experiencing the current situation in which they are becoming worse and even more extensive as we speak.

To summarize what I have been saying so far, language is often used in ways that, while well-meaning, unwittingly bring with them deficit ways of thinking that unfairly stereotype or label communities. My starting position is that, while not denying that communities that have been put at a disadvantage have problems, it makes more sense to start working with the strengths that individuals and communities possess, rather than reinforcing stereotypes that they are somehow bundles of pathologies.

The simple fact is that the playing field in which we all live is far from a level one, and for a variety of reasons some communities are simply different. They don't all look alike or conform to conventional middle-class norms and values, and an attempt to make them appear that way is likely to be a fraught process. Given their different histories, aspirations and lifestyles, these are valued communities that need to be understood and worked with on their own terms so that their inhabitants have some of the same opportunities as the rest of us for improved life chances. This is not a signal that we should be made to all look the same. Rather, what this means is that we should open up a wider range of choices and opportunities than might otherwise exist, and even be open to unconventional possibilities.

One of the features of 'community capacity building', as I am envisaging it here, is the space it provides for deeper mutual understanding between communities that are deemed 'disadvantaged' – but who proudly disavow and deny this derogatory-sounding label, because they regard themselves as arriving at their situation as a result of having had different pathways, life trajectories, opportunities, and ways of living, as well as set-backs – and those of us who constitute the dominant middle class. What I am interchangeably calling 'community capacity building' and 'community engagement' in effect amounts to a *learning space* or an *arena for possibilities* within which to work towards levelling a playing field that has been inequitably constructed in terms of access to opportunities.

One feature often prominently touted in notions of community engagement is the concept of *partnerships* – between communities deemed 'disadvantaged' and governments and agencies who believe they have an obligation to work with them. Partnerships can also be the spaces and places in which misunderstandings become glaringly apparent, as well as the interstices within which new, genuine and lasting understandings can be forged.

In order to advance this alternative view, we need a way of interrupting conventional ways of thinking about these issues. The most effective way of doing that is to present a different philosophical basis – one that is

- *relational* – in that it regards people as more important than organizations, institutions, political systems or physical structures
- *inclusive* – in that it is hospitable to the most marginalized and excluded

- *participative* – in that the community sets its own agenda and 'indigenous' (or local) leadership is fostered and encouraged
- *connected* – in its concern to build networks of association
- *socially just* – in that it is concerned with how inequities are constructed, sustained and maintained, and with how to interrupt hierarchies of privilege
- *sustainable* – in acknowledging strengths in order to build capacities for the future.

In what follows, I will broadly explore what these notions might mean.

REWORKING WHAT IS MEANT BY 'COMMUNITY CAPACITY BUILDING'

In analyzing Oxfam's relatively late arrival into the discussion of the development economics term 'capacity building', Eade (1997) explained the international NGO's reticence in these terms: 'Like most development jargon, capacity-building is now used so indiscriminately that any meaning it once had may soon evaporate. Indeed, some commentators argue that the term was never really intended to mean anything anyway and should be jettisoned' (p. 9). Notwithstanding its 'sometimes vague and inconsistent [meanings]' (p. 9), Eade (1997) argues that what lies beneath this somewhat faddish notion are a set of underlying principles for understanding and acting upon poverty that make the concept worth persisting with. Oxfam's definition portrays capacity building as being pre-eminently a 'person-centered' approach to development that underscores a number of crucial imperatives, namely, that

- . . . all people have the right to an equitable share in the world's resources, and to be the authors of their own development; and that the denial of such rights is at the heart of poverty and suffering. Strengthening people's capacity to determine their own values and priorities, and to act on these, is the basis of development. (pp. 2–3)

- Women and men, however poor or marginalized, always have many capacities, which may or may not be obvious to outsiders, and even which they themselves may not recognize. It may take time to discover these capabilities and potential. But to intervene without doing so is not only disrespectful; it also wastes an opportunity to build on these existing capacities, and – even more importantly – risks undermining them, and so leaving people even more vulnerable than they were before. (p. 3)

- . . . an individual's capacities and needs – and the opportunity to act on them – depend on the myriad factors that differentiate human beings from each other and shape social identities, relationships and life experiences . . . [Capacity building] must therefore take into account the different (and potentially negative) ways in which their impact will be felt by individuals and social groups. (p. 3)

- . . . while capacity-building is designed to promote change . . . [this] takes place within a far wider process of social and economic transformation. (p. 3)

- . . . capacity-building is not 'doing development' on the cheap, or against the clock. Nor is it risk-free. Quite the reverse. It implies a long-term investment in people and their organizations, and a commitment to the various processes through which they can better shape the forces that affect their lives. (p. 3)

The language and concepts of capacity building have their origins in the UNDP notion coined in the 1970s of 'capacitating', which refers to 'diagnosing current weaknesses and potentials, finding appropriate policies and constantly monitoring the course of development' (Eade, 1997, pp. 15–16). A close reading of Eade

(1997) reveals three major aspects to capacity building that have particular relevance for schools, their reform and the community renewal that often accompanies this in contexts of social and economic complexity.

1. Identifying Strengths and Constraints

As alluded to at various points in this book, the prevailing paradigm of school and community reform is a pathologizing one that is deficit driven: what is wrong, and what is required to fix it? In contrast, capacity building starts from the viewpoint that all communities have assets, skills and resources, but they also have constraints that limit what is possible. Strengths and constraints are not universal but differ from person-to-person and are highly context dependent. Contexts are as important as the individuals that inhabit them, and people need assistance in the identification of strengths and interferences, and in being able to see how these are not idiosyncratic, but fit into wider patterns created by social forces. One-size-fit-all approaches and 'bureaucratic impositions' (Eade, 1997, p. 19) are strenuously avoided in capacity building approaches, in favour of providing space for those most affected at the 'grass-roots level' to identify the constraints they are experiencing and, as a consequence, work towards 'realizing their basic rights' (Eade, 1997, p. 4). Put another way, quality of life is improved when those in dominant positions acknowledge that 'no one *develops* anyone else' (p. 13) and that what is required instead is to find 'appropriate vehicles through which to strengthen [people's] ability to overcome the causes of their exclusion' (p. 24). In other words, the starting point for improvements in schools and communities is for people themselves to identify the manner in which their 'choices are [being] denied' (p. 13) and how from within, together with outside support, they are able to expand the range of their access to a 'wider spectrum of capabilities' (p. 16).

114

2. Relationships-Centred and Dialogical Problem-Solving Approach

In seeking to avoid the kind of 'dependency' that is built into and that has damned reform efforts in the past, in which 'experts' administer to those who are deemed inexpert, the kind of orientation being created through capacity building is one of 'co-learning' and 'problem-solving . . . dialogue among equals' (Eade, 1997, p. 11). Having said that, while this is an approach that incorporates flexibility, it 'does not mean drifting or improvising' (p. 29). As I will indicate below, it is analytical, strategic and political, but above all it is realistic. Capacity building only works when there is a strong belief that it is important to spend considerable time 'working through problems rather than throwing money at them' (p. 26). Part of this realism is founded on the strongly held belief that for an approach to work 'it may mean starting several steps behind the "obvious" point of entry in order to avoid generating resistance' (p. 30). This is not an approach that fits well with dominant views of targets, outcomes, performance and just-in-time approaches. What we have instead is the view that if change is to be sustainable then what has to be engendered is ownership, and producing this means being 'patient and flexible' in the way in which relationships are created and sustained around authentic trust, respect and notions of mutuality and reciprocity. What this means is the creation of a 'shared reading of context' (p. 33) around a central defining agenda that is worked through in dialogical ways.

3. Analytical of Contexts and Circumstances

One of the defining features of capacity building is that it does not regard situations as being value neutral. There are always interests being served, and others being denied, excluded and marginalized. Rather than succumbing to victim-blaming mentalities, the preferred alternative is to operate on the basis of 'analysis rather than assumptions or labels' (Eade, 1997, p. 26). To that end, capacity building is not afraid of what data will reveal, because moving forward is not about apportioning blame or the preservation of image and impression management. The intent is to establish what is occurring, why, with what effects and how the resources might be organized to improve it. It is not always helpful in this to view 'the state' and 'civil society' antagonistically, as adversaries or as 'dichotomously opposed' (p. 20); rather they need to be seen and be made to operate in ways that reflect, each as being supportive of the other. Another way of putting this is that capacity-building approaches do not operate in isolation or in hermetically sealed ways. They do not exist 'in isolation from the wider social, economic and political fabric' (p. 21). Rather, capacity-building approaches are analytical of how interrelationships work and how power and influence circulate.

With the notion of capacity building, thus envisaged, we end up turning conventional views of school and community reform on their head. Those who have historically been construed as 'objects to be manipulated and controlled' are treated instead as 'creators of a learning culture' (Mitchell and Sackney, 2001, p. 1), which has an open-ended worldview that is subject to contestation, debate and negotiation. As Mitchell and Sackney (2001) put it,

> The notion of the school as a learning community represents a fundamental shift in the ideology that shapes understanding of schools and professional practice . . . a worldview . . . that is associated with a constructivist epistemology and an interpretivist methodology. This worldview positions schools and learning as generative rather than instrumental. (p. 9)

In furthering this distinction, Mitchell and Sackney (2001) envisage a constellation of 'three pivotal capacities' that are closely interrelated. First, *personal capacity* – the 'values, assumptions, beliefs and practical knowledge teachers carry with them' and their preparedness to confront these in 'com[ing] to grips with the personal narratives that shape and constrain their professional practice and learning'; that is to say, a willingness on the part of teachers to put their teaching under scrutiny in a 'search for the components of one's professional narrative (p. 3).

Second, *interpersonal capacity* – shifting the focus from the individual to the group in terms of a number of phases such as (a) 'naming and framing' the conditions of the work, (b) sharing and 'discovering the thoughts of others'; (c) confronting and deconstructing individual and group narratives so as to jointly 'reconstruct professional practice' (p. 6). Third, *organizational capacity* – building into the school the kind of structural arrangements that not only permit but also ensure that ongoing dialogue becomes a characterizing essential feature of the community and its school (p. 6).

When schools and communities take on capacity building along these lines, they are engaging in a high-risk activity as people 'put their professional identities on the line' (p. 9) in the sense of admitting that they don't know it all and that they are willing to 'expose knowledge gaps' (p. 9) and, as a consequence, to reconstruct their personal and professional identities.

These are fine aspirational ideals, but as with many ideals they get corrupted, corroded and tarnished in the pushing and shoving that occurs in the real world. In the next section, I want to turn to two things: first, the increasing slippage, drifting and hijacking of *community capacity building*; and second, a move towards *community organizing* approaches.

COMMUNITY CAPACITY BUILDING: CONTESTED, CONFLICTUAL, CONGENITAL?

It is not difficult to see why hardened community-based practitioners are attracted to terms such as community capacity building. As Smith et al. (2001) put it, 'when faced with the daily pressures to provide education and services to people accustomed to having government "do for" them' it is not hard to 'join the growing chorus of those who argue that community capacity building is our future' (p. 30). In seeking to put clarity on what is a murky and obfuscated term, Smith et al. (2001) say that community capacity building is about 'foster[ing] *initiation* of actions by community members . . . a process of working with a community to determine what its needs and strengths are, and to develop ways of using those strengths to meet those needs' (p. 31). From their scoping of a variety of literatures, Smith et al. (2001) define community capacity building as 'the degree to which a community can develop, implement and sustain actions . . . [which allow it] . . . to exert greater control over their physical, social, economic and cultural environments' (p. 33). Pointing to the schizophrenic nature of community capacity building, Verity (2007) presents it as variously being 'elusive', 'slippery', 'shifting', 'contested', 'muddled' and 'ill defined' (Chapman and Kirk, 2001, pp. 7–8), while at the same time being 'exciting', 'innovative', 'empowering', 'significant' and 'new'" (Verity, 2007). For its most ardent advocates, community capacity building presents an amalgam of alleged benefits, which I will present in summary form, for reasons of brevity, as follows:

- Empowerment of individuals and groups within defined 'communities'
- Development of skills, knowledge, and confidence
- Increased social connections and relationships
- Responsive service delivery and policy based in community identified needs and solutions
- Audible community voices
- Community involvement
- Responsive and accountable decision makers
- Resource mobilization for communities in need
- Community acceptance of programs because they have been involved in their development. (Verity, 2007, p. 11)

At the commonsense level of attributes such as these, community building appears to be as an innocuous sounding ideal that is difficult to oppose, and may be equally difficult to dislodge, and maybe that is what is intended. In the social discourses of health, education and welfare, notions of community are a major policy relay. Makuwira (2007a) argues that in order to make sense of community capacity building as a public policy initiative, and to reveal its real agenda, we need to examine something of its 'political economy' (p. 129) to see what it is up to.

In order to put the notion of 'community' as it is being deployed in the public policy context under scrutiny, I want to start by invoking some of its major critics.

If what follows appears to be somewhat derivative, it is for good reason – I am trying to marshal and present the arguments in order to begin to explore an alternative. Over two decades ago, Bryson and Mowbray (1981) argued that the term 'community' had become the new 'spray-on solution' for protracted social problems, and its policy appeal has escalated significantly since then. Since Bryson and Mowbray's analysis in the early 1980s, there has been an explosion in the popularity of government-inspired usage of the term community, including 'community/capacity building, government-community partnerships and community and neighborhood renewal' (Mowbray, 2005, p. 255). Bryson and Mowbray regard the resurgence of community as a 'vogue idea in policy discourse' (Mowbray, 2005, p. 255) that has become 'ideologically driven' (Bryson and Mowbray, 2005, p. 91). This ideological deployment of 'community' as a linguistic tool has been joined by 'social capital' as part of a wider government strategy to provide 'apparently cheaper community based services, while purporting to imply much more' (p. 91). In an editorial introduction to the *Community Development Journal*, Craig (2003) summarized this tendency when he said, 'This may be good news in general, but it generates concern amongst the community development community' (p. 2).

The reason for the alarm seems to lie, therefore, in the unac-knowledged limitations of 'the capacity of local communi-ties to act autonomously and to express their needs free from "shaping" by the interests of government' (Craig, 2003, p. 2). At the core are legitimate 'questions about why governments have such enthusiasm for community development in the first place' (p. 2). Within the 'murky and confused' language are unanswered questions about the provision of services that may 'barely [be] related to the needs identified by local communi-ties' (Craig, 2003, p. 2).

The game of rhetorical flourish being played here seems, therefore, to be one of ascribing 'positive qualities to community' as a way of 'depoliticiz[ing] social problems' (Mowbray, 2005, p. 257). In other words, ascribing a sense of quasi-causation to urban or industrial systems rather than to 'a class society and the capitalist political order . . . allows solutions [to be] couched in technical, rather then explicitly political terms' (Bryson and Mowbray, 1981, p. 56). The reality is that so-called 'bottom-up' programmes are really state funded, controlled and regulated, albeit within a discourse that celebrates 'local autonomy and other communitarian values' (Mowbray, 2005, p. 257). It seems that the language game is one of invoking wholesome-sounding words like 'community' to convey the outward appearances of being 'caring, responsive and progressive' (p. 257). Mowbray (2005) says the situation is made even more compelling if the full range of warm, fuzzy terms are invoked, such as 'shared values', 'shared identity', 'reciprocity', 'trust', 'equity', 'cohesion', 'inclusion' and 'social capital' (p. 257). The real intent seems to be to use a progressive discourse to veil a cost-cutting agenda by the state. At another level, the contradictory, blurred and confused terminology places the 'most onerous obligations on the most disadvantaged individuals' (Cass and Brennan, 2002, p. 259) in a context in which the 'localist rhetoric' effectively provides a 'smokescreen for underlying opposition to effective collective action or community advocacy' (Mowbray, 2005, p. 258). The 'systematic de-funding of community groups' (Cass and Brennan, 2002, p. 253) that accompanies this community turn and the presentation of a notion of community in seemingly 'neutral' terms 'devoid of contested politics' amounts to a situation that is either 'curiously non-reflective, or mischievous in the extreme' (Cass and Brennan, 2002, p. 249).

For Mowbray (2004), the most significant drawback of community capacity building lies in the way its ardent advocates are 'exultant' (p. 18) to the point of refusing to confront and learn from its failures. While the virtues of not being 'top down' are talked up, advocates studiously avoid analysis of the tensions, dilemmas, contradictions and perplexities in favour of 'a predominantly local frame of reference, and inward focus and consensual activities, albeit with relatively grandiose ambitions for achievement' (p. 18). The effect of this 'overwhelming consensual' approach that actively discourages discord, dissent and contention is that 'community activism' around issues of social justice are made 'invisible' (Mowbray, 2004, p. 19). Carson (2004) has noted that such victim-blaming approaches avoid 'structural' (p. 17) explanations to deep-seated social problems.

All the hype around the concept of community capacity building obscures the way the concept is 'covertly used to subjugate and create [a] power imbalance between the "builders" (supposedly those with the power) and the "beneficiaries" (those assumed to be powerless)' (Makuwira, 2007a, p. 129). What gets to be avoided are important questions, such as

What is capacity? Who needs capacity? Capacity to do what? Whose interest(s) is/are served when people's capacities are built? Who determines the process and with what effects? Who evaluates and ascertains that capacity has been achieved? (Makuwira, 2007b, p. 129)

121

These are questions that remain curiously silent in the community capacity building discourse. Where the concern becomes most glaringly apparent is over ownership and the assumption that 'initiatives will be owned by local communities' (Makuwira, 2007a, p. 134). This can take on a delusional quality, and we do ourselves a disservice when we embrace ideas like community capacity building uncritically, especially when they have been co-opted by the neoconservative agenda Brown (2003) labels 'the tricky trio' – 'devolution', 'privatization' and 'community building'. As she put it, 'taken together, they are strategies for shifting the burden of social responsibility from the public to the private sphere' (p. 1). In her paper *Community Building in Difficult Times*, Brown (2003) identifies several threats to a more authentic view of community capacity building, which Cass and Brennan (2002) identify as a misreading of disadvantage. As they put it,

> individuals and communities are not naturally disadvantaged, their disadvantage is economically, politically and socially constructed by the operations of financial markets, labour markets and housing markets and by government economic and public policies. (p. 257)

What clearly needs to be addressed are 'the underlying market and policy causes of these unequal spatially concentrated distributions of income, capital and employment opportunities' (Cass and Brennan, 2002, p. 257).

The line of argument I am pursuing here is that the notion of community capacity building is at essence a deficit category situated in a distorted nostalgic recollection. If we take the Putnam (2000) argument in his internationally acclaimed *Bowling Alone*, that western countries are experiencing a depletion of social capital, then as Brown (2003) puts it, the argument is founded on a partial and deceptively misleading recollection of white, middle–class, US males (p. 2). What gets excluded in Putnam's apolitical kind of analysis is the notion that poor and working-class communities of difference may not experience this depletion, or at least not in the way being envisaged and portrayed by Putnam. Brown (2003) argues that community engagement is markedly different from what it was several decades ago, 'as the disparity between rich and poor . . . continues to grow uncontrollably' (p. 2); most notably,

> People in poverty are engaged with food banks and homeless shelters. The working poor are engaged in parenting programs and budgeting courses in order to keep the state out of its families. The dwindling middle classes are engaged in Oprah reading clubs, investment groups and exercise gyms. (p. 2)

Brown's (2003) argument is really pointing us to the middle-classness of notions of community capacity building, community engagement and social capital as they are conventionally being framed. Such a view elides the existential and differential forms of engagement across different classes. In particular, it falls short on the question of 'how we are "in relation" with one another', and in this Brown questions whether the most appropriate response is one of extending 'charitable works' and whether we want to be 'in relation' with community in ways 'where some of us get to be benevolent and others are expected to be grateful' (p. 2).

What Brown (2003) regards as being implicit within conservative views of community building, and hence a threat to the alternative she labels 'relational community building' and its points of departure, are

- *self-interest* – which is to say, how possessive, individualistic competition corrupts and corrodes the larger ideal that when community is better off, we all gain. By way of contrast, *relational community building* thinks and acts in integrated ways.
- *disparity* – the notion that as inequality grows, then so too does the inability of some groups and individuals to engage in a

range of activities. *Relational community building* starts with questions about how the most excluded might be included.

- tension around *inclusion and exclusion* – consensus is not only unattainable in diverse communities, but it comes at the considerable expense of silencing some voices and sustaining the status quo. *Relational community building* acknowledges and allows for 'a plethora of ideas and strategies . . . between often very disparate groups' (Brown, 2003, p. 2).

- *denial of history, cheating social justice* – there is acknowledgement of the often buried reality that not everyone starts from the same place and that the playing field is far from level. *Relational community building* foregrounds historical oppression and seeks to deal with inequities by asking 'how do our community building actions maintain or challenge inequalities?' (Brown, 2003, p. 4) – for example, by actively challenging hierarchies of 'racism, homophobia, ableism, classism' and gender (p. 4).

- *complacency* – privilege and inequality breed feelings of hopelessness, that it is all too hard, and that the solution lies elsewhere and is somebody else's problem. *Relational community building* punctures this myth by repositioning it as everyone's problem.

Smith et al. (2001) bring together what a reworked notion of community in a context of relationships means when they say,

> We believe in the vital importance of strengthening these interpersonal relations. Yet while we see community as a central unit for analysis and action, we do not make the naive assumption that community can do no wrong. There are divisions and differences within any community, relationships of power and privilege, disempowerment and deprivation. Good community development means identifying and wrestling with these deeply political issues. (p. 34)

HOW IS THE 'COMMUNITY ORGANIZING' APPROACH TO SCHOOL REFORM DIFFERENT?

What lies at the heart of the community organizing approach is 'relational power' (Warren, 2004; 2005; Smyth 2006a,b), or what Stone, Doherty and Ross (1999) call a 'social production model of power' (p. 354). As they put it,

> society is characterized mainly by a lack of coherence, not by a single system of domination and subordination. Society is a loose network of institutional arrangements . . . In this kind of loosely joined society 'the issue is how to bring enough co-operation among disparate community elements to get things done.' (Stone, 1989, p. 227)

This is 'power to' rather than 'power over' (p. 354). While much has been written about community organizing (Sanders, 1970; Boyte, 1980; Delgado, 1986; Horwitt, 1989; Williams, 1989; Shirley, 1997; 2002; Gittell and Vidal, 1998; Warren, 2001; Warren and Wood, 2001; Osterman, 2002; Wood, 2002; Chambers with Cowan, 2004; Gecan, 2004; Oakes and Rogers with Lipton, 2006; Orr, 2007), its essence lies in building power that results in social justice. Makuwira (2007b) summarizes its contemporary principles as follows:

Participation . . . 'as an end in itself . . . particularly through . . . knowledge building, and being responsible custodians'

Inclusiveness . . . drawing into the decision making processes diverse communities especially those placed at 'the periphery of decision-making processes'

Scope of Mission and Vision . . . the requirement for 'clear and precise aims and goals' that embrace 'broader issues that affect the community rather than being narrowly focused'

Critical Perspective . . . which is to say, 'advocating for positive policy and institutional change' that is conducive to 'active participation', 'ownership' and 'accountability and transparency in organizations and institutions that marginalize people'. (pp. 383–4 emphases in original)

There can never be any guarantee of success with such approaches, but the considerable advantage of this approach over community capacity building is that it provides a circuit-breaker to the removal of a major obstacle:

> Though the process need not be fully conscious, social production can be a matter of bringing about a fresh configuration of preferences through opening up new possibilities. The effort may not succeed . . . but success means putting people in different relationships with one another and that in turn means bringing together sufficient resources to pursue a broadly defined purpose. (Stone et al., 1999, p. 354)

One of the merits of community organizing is that the approach is upfront about issues of power. Warren (2004) says a major impediment among educators is their wariness to talk about issues of power. He says,

> educators are particularly uncomfortable with discussions about power, compared to other institutional leaders with whom community organizations interact. Principals and teachers oftentimes feel disempowered themselves even as they hold considerable authority over students and therefore unilateral power over low-income families. Principals can be narrowly protectionist and suspicious of community demands. Emphasizing relational power might help provide an entree to schools educators who are uneasy with discussions of power and the realities of conflict. (p. 6)

126

In this Warren (2004) makes the useful distinction between three types of community-school collaboration:

- the 'service model' most commonly found in the concept of 'full service schools' that adopt a neighborhood centre and 'integrated provision of education, health and other services to children and adults' (p. 6)
- the 'development model' as embodied in the notion of 'community sponsorship of new schools' (e.g. charter schools) which amount to partnerships to provide community-based forms of education
- the 'organizing model' in which the fundamental commitment is to 'school-community organizing' committed to the 'development of leadership and power to change schools and improve communities'. (p. 6)

These are substantively and qualitatively different entities in a period of 'experimentation in an emerging field of school-community collaboration' (Warren, 2004, p. 32), and I want to now make some comments on the latter.

THE RELEVANCE OF A COMMUNITY ORGANIZING APPROACH TO SCHOOL REFORM IN CONTEXTS OF DISADVANTAGE

As Australian education moves to embrace the rhetoric of social inclusion – not unlike other countries, such as the United Kingdom – along with its apparatuses of a Social Inclusion Unit and Social Inclusion Board, the term 'community' and 'community capacity building' are coming to be increasingly invoked as a major policy weapon. What seems to lie at the heart of this is the view noted by Nash and Christie (2003), in respect of the UK experience, that 'monitoring and improving the quality of people's social relationships' is coming to be regarded by government 'as a way of relieving poverty or reducing cultural tensions' (p. i). In Victoria we can see this, for example, in the Government's recently released blueprint for early childhood development and school reform (Department of Education and Early Childhood Development, 2008), with its 'strengthening partnerships with parents and communities' in which the undefined term 'community' is invoked 56 times and the opaque notion of 'partnerships' 48 times in the three-part discussion paper. The broader policy trajectory labeled a 'Fairer Victoria' within which the educational agenda sits also reflects this infatuation, with 'capacity' building mentioned 86 times and 'community' 1,061 times in four relatively short policy documents (State Government of Victoria, 2005a,b; 2006a,b). This conveys a powerful message about how both the 'problem' and the 'solution' are being officially framed.

We can see these same tendencies at the level of the Australian federal government. Given the admiration former Prime Minister Kevin Rudd and present Prime Minister Julia Gillard both have for the Blair government's social policies, it is not surprising to find that Tom Bentley, a former Blair adviser, had been appointed to work with then Deputy Prime Minister Julia Gillard in establishing a Social Inclusion Unit. It will come as no surprise either to see the Australian government borrowing and 'adapting ideas from Blair' (Nader, 2008, p. 6) in handling social disadvantage. It is appropriate, therefore, to ask what lessons there might be for Australia from the UK experience. Blair (2002) left no doubt as to where his emphasis was: 'Community is the governing idea of modern social democracy' (p. 9). 'Our aim should be to give voice to our communities and to transform aspirations into practical programs' (p. 13). Where the concern lies in proclamations like these is that the notion of 'community' being borrowed is highly derivative of Third World development projects, such as UNDP, that have become 'better known for fiscal conservatism than for political and social risk-taking [and

this has] frequently led . . . to the undermining of local community social and economic structures whilst appearing to advocate
the importance of "community"' (Craig, 2007, p. 339). There
appears to be scant regard given here to 'issues of social justice'
(Craig, 2007, p. 339).

From a public policy perspective, far from notions of community and partnerships being benign and benevolent, they are actually constitutive of a much wider 'reconfiguring [of] the state' that
is well underway (McDonald and Marston, 2002, p. 6). Putting
the argument in its sharpest form, McDonald and Marston say
that the rhetoric of this new institutional game positions the
notion of 'community' 'as the ideal site for meeting social needs
and constructing ideal citizens, while the state accepts an increasingly residual function' (p. 6). What this new discourse of policy
governance constitutes, they argue, is 'a highly seductive set of
legitimizing rhetorics' (p. 6) that border on the irresistible. All the
right kinds of noises are made about the need for the meddle-
some state to get out of the way and allow individuals to control
their own lives. What we have in this kind of wholesome rhetoric
is an 'obscuring effect' which laminates over what the 'enabling
state' is really up to: 'The rhetorical implication is that within this
space citizens are somehow "free" from government instrumen-
talities that are associated with the oppressive and disabling state'
(McDonald and Marston, 2002, p. 8). What remains undisclosed,
of course, is what comes with the new rhetorical meanings around
community, namely, that it is deeply 'implicated in a conservative
politics which serve to minimize state responsibility for the support
of a whole range of life course dependencies' (p. 7). Appropriately
shrouded and obfuscated is 'the central individualist and contrac-
tual core of the new regime of welfare' (p. 7). Especially troubling
is the fact that this new policy discourse brings with it 'entirely new
meanings and norms of control that are fundamentally at odds
with principles of social justice' (p. 7). The kind of 'naturalized
perception' (p. 8) of wholesome goodness attached to concepts

such as 'civic engagement', 'community capacity building' and 'sustainable communities' (p. 8) are ones that in the end

> shift away from a focus on material inequalities, becoming fix-
> ated [instead] on patterns of 'inclusion' and 'exclusion'. In turn,
> this transforms the problem of poverty . . . into one that has less
> to do with material and cultural resources [and more to do]
> with a lack of belonging. (p. 8)

The ultimate effect, then, is to preserve the conditions that created the unequal order in the first place so that 'the social and economic processes that generate such phenomenon as poverty, homeless-ness, inequality and violence are left largely out of the equation' (McDonald and Marston, 2002, p. 8).

It is difficult, therefore, to avoid the conclusion arrived at by McDonald and Marston (2002) that what we have being enacted in the largely unspecified notions of community is a 'new insti-tutional order' that is being constructed as 'a space or niche' to be conveniently filled at precisely the point at which the state is retreating from its historical responsibilities in what is unquestion-ably 'an extremely turbulent, unstable and highly contested envi-ronment' (p. 3).

It is appropriate that I bring discussion back to schools, and I will do so through the lens of 'community organizing for school reform' (Mediratta et al., 2001; Zachary and olatoye, 2001; Gold and Simon with Brown, 2002; Mediratta et al., 2002; 2003; 2008; Warren, 2004; 2007; Smith, 2007). For starters, the notion of *parental engagement* is qualitatively different from the conventional view of *parental involvement* in schooling (Gold and Simon with Brown, 2005).

Parental involvement is a category that has largely been the crea-ture of neo-liberal policy reform trajectories that have for the past 30 years constructed parents as individualist, rational, self-seeking consumers who are highly adept at making so-called 'choices'. The driving idea behind the neo-liberal view is that parents will be involved in the schooling of their children because they want to maximize the 'valued added' aspect of schooling for their offspring. Accordingly, they will search for the 'best deal' or, in the official language, 'exercise school choice' and in general muscle schools to make them accountable for outcomes, under conditions of duress and threat of withdrawal of patronage. The intent is to ensure that, to the greatest extent possible, schools deliver a 'service' in the form of making children more saleable in the employment market. This view of 'parents as partners for improvement' (Gold and Simon with Brown, 2005, p. 242) is one that some of us find manipulative and exploitative because of the way it positions parents as passive 'clients'. Gold and Simon with Brown (2005) argue that an 'expanded role for parents in their children's education' is laudable at one level, but it comes at the expense of perpetrating 'a focus on parents as listeners and supporters, rather than as advocates for equity or decision-makers' (p. 242).

The notion of *parental engagement*, or to put it another way 'parents in community', goes considerably beyond taking an interest in and supporting the school for what it will return in terms of individual educational capital. Parental engagement is predicated on a socially activist, collectivist, socially critical, equity-oriented and community-minded view of participation that is committed to improving the learning of all students in the community, not just the few. This is an approach that is located in a 'citizen politics' (Boyte, 1989) or a 'relational view of politics', as I put it in *Activist and Socially Critical School and Community Renewal* (Smyth et al., 2009), that foregrounds ideas of *Social Justice and the Politics of Community* (Everingham, 2003).

In making and pursuing this distinction, I am not merely making a semantic point – what I have in mind goes to the heart of the place of schools in public life. As Keith (1999) put it,

the problem with conventional models of parental involvement is not merely . . . their 'deficit' approach to parents. It is that

131

schools, by treating parents, students and community members as clients and consumers are reneging on their historic responsibility as sites for education in democracy and thus further contributing to the erosion of public life. This is a serious issue at a time when public disengagement from politics and public institutions is already high. (p. 230)

Community organizing for school reform is, therefore, concerned with 'the democratization of both governance structures and the curriculum of schools' (Gold and Simon with Brown, 2005, p. 242). What needs to be engendered and extended, Gold et al. (2005) argue, is 'social trust' – by which they mean 'power to' rather than 'power over' (p. 243). In other words, parental involvement on its own can be shallow, synthetic and manipulative of parents, teachers and students when the aim is personal gain or raising the public relations image of the school. What is needed instead are 'accountable relationships' that are based on 'trust . . . established through . . . mutual agreement about . . . obligations to one another' (p. 243).

It is important to say that there are many variants of community organizing and that Australia has not been without its hybridized homegrown varieties, albeit ones that have tended to galvanize around particular issues at strategic historical moments. For example, during the 1970s in Sydney around the struggles of the Builders Laborers Federation in heritage and cultural preservation, in Adelaide and Melbourne around the creation of women's shelters, and nationally in the Disadvantaged Schools Program. At other moments, local examples can be found in the struggles against the Kennett government in Victoria in the 1990s against school closures and the community schools movement in the 1970s. Aboriginal communities have a long history of community organizing in order to obtain services. In many of these instances, key figures were trained in the approach of 1920s American activist Saul Alinsky (1989a,b). While it is not easy to briefly summarize Alinsky's 'method', there are four orienting principles (for elaboration, see Smyth, 2006b; Smyth et al., 2009): (a) relational immediacy, or the importance of face-to-face relationships; (b) indigenous leadership through enabling communities to foster locally developed leaders; (c) interdependency in the sense of forming coalitions and alliances; and (d) seeing the 'bigger picture' in terms of wider structural issues that produce inequality.

There is not a strong tradition of Alinsky-type community organizing approaches to educational reform, although there are growing indications (Thomson, 2005) that this could be an extremely helpful new direction. The notion of community organizing for school reform can be regarded as operating through a carefully thought-out strategic political relay that involves a number of what Gold and Simon with Brown (2005) refer to as 'indicator areas' that are activated to bring about change in schools through two cornerstones or 'building blocks'.

The first cornerstone is 'building community capacity', and unlike some of its lookalikes spoken about earlier, it involves several deliberate processes, around *leadership development* (educating parents and community members so they can see how power works, how to negotiate, how to formulate and pursue broad change agenda for schools, how to work out why some children are excluded and generally helping them to see how they can work collectively in more politically savvy ways); *community power* (helping residents act together so as to strategically acquire resources necessary to improve school contexts, how to analyse inequities and lack of transparency, and how to confront official obstinacy and inertia); *social capital* (helping to bring together broad networks and getting them to see their mutual interests, helping them to form the 'bridging relationships' (p. 245) necessary for sustained change, and enabling them to engender the kind of trust necessary among diverse constituencies that may not even know one another).

The second cornerstone is 'school improvement', not in the conservative technical or instrumental sense of that term, but rather of a kind that comprises a constellation of pressure points capable of leading to improved learning for students, including the press for *equity* (securing increased funding and resources with which to redress inequities, expanding the cultural range of educational opportunities for students, ensuring that teaching and learning are culturally appropriate and responsive); pushing forward *school/community connections* (where both are regarded as a resource or an asset for use by the other and together, and where parents have multiple roles and opportunities in the school and the community); *school climate* (where there is an enduring culture of high expectations and rigorous teaching and learning among teachers as well as students, where learning experiences are interesting and built around student and community interests, and where pedagogy and curriculum reflect this).

The bridging or integrating concept that holds the cornerstones of *community capacity building and school improvement* in productive tension is what Gold et al. (2005) label *public accountability* – this is not in any way related to the neo-liberal process of naming and shaming schools. Quite the contrary, public accountability is a kind of space within which commitments are entered into publicly, closely monitored and followed through to 'solve the problems of public education' (p. 245). They are not instances in which solutions are demanded of government officials so much as they are a working out of how problems might be framed, the resources required to advance on them and the appropriate political strategy to ensure that those publicly responsible deliver on promises and agreements. In short, this is a manifestation of what is meant by the notion of 'collective responsibility' (p. 245). It necessarily encompasses aspects such as having the conversation about why there is an educational achievement gap, how to frame it in ways other than blaming the victim, how polices and programmes can be made to address these inequities and, above all, what might be achieved through 'joint ownership/relational culture' (p. 250).

A PLACE IN WHICH TO START RATHER THAN FINISH – WHEN IT COMES TO COMMUNITY ENGAGEMENT

A way of drawing this chapter together might be to share something of a process and some working principles that my colleagues and I (Smyth et al., 2011) have used in pursuing the topic *What to Look for in Genuine Community Engagement*.

There are three things that need to be brought to this kind of agenda.

First is to do what I have already been doing at some length in this chapter in *puncturing some of the enduring and deficit-ridden mythologies* surrounding what is involved in working with communities deemed to be 'disadvantaged'.

Second is to move beyond merely noting and critiquing deficit perspectives and *bringing into focus action questions* that provide a basis for *the development of local leadership initiatives*, such as

- Who is community engagement for?
- Who gets to speak?
- Who is driving the idea of community engagement?
- Is it deeply enough embedded in local leadership to be sustainable? How do we avoid coercing people – or how to we get real connectedness?

These are broad framing or orienting questions of a kind that, if we can create and sustain the kind of safe dialogical spaces in which they can be openly and honestly pursued, will enable even quite diverse communities to see what is happening, while at the same time developing local alternatives which they own. Implicit within these questions are some underlying commitments towards being

- *relational* – in regarding people as more important than organizations, institutions, political systems or physical structures
- *inclusive* – in being hospitable to the most marginalized and excluded
- *participative* – in that the community sets its own agenda and where 'indigenous' (or local) leadership is fostered and encouraged
- *connected* – in having a concern to build networks of association
- *socially just* – dealing with how inequities get to be constructed, sustained and maintained, and how to interrupt hierarchies of privilege
- *sustainable* – in acknowledging strengths that exist in communities in order to build capacities for the future.

Third is to pursue a process that provides the dialogical space in which 'outsiders' and 'community members' can engage in some genuine listening. We have called this 'community voiced' or 'listening' (from the position of the experts) process a *Community Centred Action Research* approach, and it has a series of staged phases or moments to it that are given schematically in Figure 4.1.

The crucial point of departure for the approach of community engagement I am suggesting is the question, whose views are valued and whose prevail? In deficit approaches, even ones that are carefully veiled or masked, there is a very clear hierarchy – those who believe they 'know' and have the right to know, and are called 'experts', and those who are considered to be 'defective' or 'deficient' and are by definition 'inexpert'. The latter are supposed to be grateful beneficiaries of the activities of the former.

The way it generally works under these sets of arrangements is that inexperts get 'spoken to' or 'talked over'. Outsiders bring with them their 'welfare' or 'management-speak', which is an alien

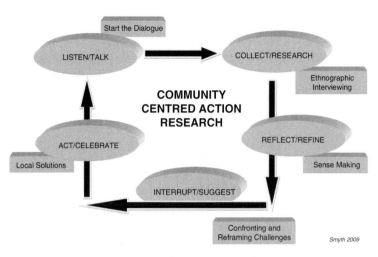

Figure 4.1 Community-Centred Action Research.

and alienating discourse. Residents, if they are involved at all, are involved only 'tokenistically' – at best they are 'consulted' – or 'informed' as to what is 'best' for them. If there is an attempt to involve residents in decisions about things affecting their lives, it is a thinly veiled form of manipulation designed to keep them compliant. Attempts to involve residents are often hermetically sealed in the sense that they are quarantined to 'safe areas', dealing with less significant issues or the implementation of decisions taken elsewhere. The effect is to create a situation of continued dependence.

Another quite different starting point might be to consider the outsiders to be 'non-experts' in the sense of having 'answers' or 'solutions'. If we think about the role of the 'outsider' in these terms, then it becomes clear that the function is not about being an 'expert'. Rather, it is more about

- starting *dialogue* among people and setting up amenable conditions
- *eliciting, collecting, researching* and bringing together views from as many diverse viewpoints as possible

- *reflecting, refining and making sense* of what is being spoken about
- interrupting, suggesting, confronting and helping people to reframe challenges
- helping to bring into existence *local solutions* and actions and ensuring that successes are *recognized and celebrated.*

Prominent here is the issue of working through difficulties with communities so as to arrive at new understandings, while no one is afraid to ask difficult questions.

The phases or moments in this kind of community engagement approach do not lend themselves to superficial or quick application, then exit – it may take several months of careful relational work, involving the following steps.

LISTEN/TALK

This is the first and most crucial aspect, in which the basis of trust is established. This is the point at which the underpinning relational conditions can be made or broken. A way of doing this and establishing authenticity as an honest broker and outside 'advocate' is to convene a *Community Listening Conference*. These conferences presuppose and require a good deal of relational work with the key people in the community, and having them delivers a range of community members prepared to come to the listening event. This is where a good deal of goodwill is drawn upon in convincing people that this is a genuine attempt to hear grass-roots views – and not some orchestrated event run by and for the benefit of outsiders. The design is along the lines of a town-hall meeting, in which there is no agenda other than to listen to whatever happens to be on the community's mind. This might be framed up a little, with some guiding questions, such as the following:

- What are the real strengths of your community?
- Why is this a good place in which to live?
- What makes it that way?
- What could be done to make your community even better?
- What gets in the way of making improvements?
- How do you (might you) get around these obstacles?
- What would you like to know more about with regard to your community?

To make these venues a relatively safe place in which people feel comfortable to speak, the *Listening Conference* needs to be in a small round-table format of 5–6 people per table, with one member who agrees to act as a scribe for the main points that emerge, and either that person or someone else elected to report more widely on the essence of the discussion to a plenary session of the Conference. Such sessions need to be of relatively short duration, around 15 minutes, membership of the groups needs to change frequently and a guiding question should be provided to focus discussion in each session. There might be four of these sessions in the course of a half-day conference – leaving time for people to socialize informally over coffee or tea.

From the records of the group recorders and our own reflections and notes, as organizers of these sessions, we develop a list of the general impressions of the major directions that have emerged from the listening event, to be used later to help us in interpreting what has been occurring and to get a sense of the stability of the issues raised and that might appear in other parts of the community engagement process.

COLLECT/RESEARCH

This is the point at which the process reaches a little deeper into the issues that surfaced at the *Listening Conference*. It is the opportunity to invite people to have one-on-one discussions with us as outside conveners or facilitators, or to have discussions in pairs or small groups if they prefer, to tell us in more detail something about the themes that emerged from the *Listening Conference*.

We make it clear that differing interpretations are welcome, that we are not passing judgements, and that there are no right and wrong answers – merely the opportunity to lead us into the complexities and variations in whatever way people are prepared to.

Our own preference, with appropriate assurances and permissions about ethical confidentiality, is to make partial transcripts of these conversations – in our case, *in situ*, using a fast typist working on a laptop – but only after we have fully explained the process to informants. In its full explication, we call this *ethnographic interviewing*, because we are still trying to understand the lives and cultures of the community we are working with.

REFLECT/REFINE

As in any situation of volatility and complexity, there is a need to withdraw periodically in order to do some deep thinking, organizing, thematizing and strategizing in relation to what has been occurring. We regard this *sense making* as being an indispensable part of an authentic community engagement process. It is the space in which a reflective surface is developed upon which to draw, before suggestions or changes are proffered. This is a stage that is completely missing from almost all attempts to alter what is occurring in contexts deemed to be 'disadvantaged', and it is the single most significant reason (along with an inability to listen) that community renewal efforts fail.

This stepping back is a significant way of refining and reframing what has been learned through a community-owned learning process, albeit one facilitated by outside critical friends.

Although this *sense making* is being done by us as facilitators, it is not done in monastic isolation, because the next stage involves drawing these reflections back into a grass-roots dialogue in a community forum that reveals in summary what has apparently been learned so far, along with possible strategies and options that might be considered for change. These options are embedded in and emerge from the 'listenings' from the *Listening Conference and the ethnographic interviewing*. The veracity of these are robustly tested as we re-present what we have heard to the community forum. The particular tone we try to develop at this point is one that focuses on a number of action items, which leads us to . . .

INTERRUPT/SUGGEST

The whole notion of change is predicated on bringing about a degree of unsettlement or unhappiness with the existing state of affairs and interrupting that with alternative suggestions. This is certainly not a process for the faint-hearted, because it involves a preparedness to challenge, confront and eventually reframe things – and this demands courage, leadership, passion, persistence and vision.

So, this stage of genuine community engagement involves putting out ideas for community debate that have surfaced from the earlier stages and managing the debates with various interest groups, but in a way in which the core issue is prominently foregrounded and not allowed to dissipate or get lost – that is to say, how whatever is occurring is demonstrably working to improve the life chances and opportunities of the community concerned.

This can be a volatile, contentious and untidy part of the process – but it is the ultimate test, too, of the authenticity of what is being attempted here – and whether ideas can be debated (as distinct from personalities attacked) in a way in which the force of argument is eventually allowed to prevail.

The end point is the collection of suggestions for action that most people can agree to live with – which does then lead us into the final aspect.

ACT/CELEBRATE

Probably one of the most important and culminating aspects of the community engagement process that we are advocating and championing here is the notion of *local solutions* – the idea that communities of disadvantage are indeed profound witnesses of the predicaments they find themselves in, as well as important repositories of ideas about what needs to be done.

This is not to deny that significant assistance and resources are required in order to change the often entrenched circumstances of disadvantage – that is not in dispute. More to the point is the fact that these communities need to be part of the 'solution', crafting ideas in collaboration with outsiders, but having a significant stake in putting them into place. This approach is a million miles away from being regarded as bundles of pathologies and needing to be the grateful recipients of other people's solutions. It is not only putting out solutions that are owned and crafted by communities, assisted by outsiders, but celebrating the importance of this as well.

NOTE

1 I am grateful to Tim Harrison for drawing this book to my attention.

CHAPTER 5

Continuing the Struggle . . . Pursuing the *Light on the Hill* through a Conversation with Joe Kincheloe

It is nonsense to speak about bringing a volume like this to a 'conclusion' when there is so much inequality and injustice in the world, and both of these are worsening by the day. The struggle for social justice has barely begun, and sometimes I fear we are heading backwards at an accelerating pace. My reference to 'the light on the hill' is to a phrase coined by Australian Labour Prime Minister Ben Chifley in 1949, and it has resonated down through the years as a metaphor for those who struggle to advance and keep alive socially just ideas in dark and dangerous times.

As I look back over the essays I have selected for this book, written at various points over the past 30 years or so, I realize the extent to which each one of them has been inspired in one way or another by Paulo Freire's *Pedagogy of the Oppressed*. While I did not use Paulo's book as a constant reference text in my own writing, there can be no doubt that it was always profoundly there in the background, with its big ideas continually inspiring, shaping and informing my thinking and my work.

As I sat down to write this final piece, I received a copy of a testament to an incredible colleague and close friend, and his enduring body of work that was tragically cut short with his death on 19 December 2008. It is a body of scholarship and research that epitomizes, in the contemporary context, what Paulo Freire truly stood for – it was *Key Works in Critical Pedagogy: Joe L. Kincheloe* (hayes et al., 2011). I was privileged to be one of the 16 contributors to that volume invited to revisit one of Joe's key works and engage in a conversation with it – it was a remarkable experience, made even more so now that I can see the pieces written by the other contributors and the contextualization of each piece by Shirley Steinberg, Joe's partner and companion in everything.

While it is not going to be possible in the short space of this chapter to do justice to all of Joe's ideas and the way many of us have collectively intersected and engaged with them, Joe would have eschewed anything that looked even vaguely like a compendium of his ideas. He would have been delighted with the notion of continuing the conversation in the robust way in which he led his own forthright life.

There can be no better way to draw together the ideas I have been struggling with here than to bring them into brief conversation with the remarkable body of work that represents Joe Kincheloe's lifetime project of critical pedagogy.

Seeing what others have come to view as important and salient in Joe's thinking and writing about critical pedagogy has been a salutary experience for me in reading *Key Works*, and I can think of no more apposite way of drawing Joe into this conversation than to invoke some of the ideas contained in that collection dedicated to Joe. It is not so much what we have collectively learned *from* Joe, for he would find such a transmission view anathema, but rather what we have learned *with* Joe that I want to highlight.

The problem with a monumental body of work like that created by Joe Kincheloe is that it is extraordinarily difficult to know how or where to enter into or emerge from it. In Joe's case, this task is made somewhat easier because of the enduring glue that held his lifetime project together and which he liked to call an 'evolving criticality' – it is multifaceted and multi-fronted, and is certainly not something that can be hermetically sealed or neatly rolled out in a rational, linear fashion.

At the expense of doing Joe an enormous disservice – and those who know me well have long ago forgiven me for my penchant and predisposition to always try to render things in a way that, while not dumbing them down, seeks rather to make complexity accessible – what I have produced is a synoptic or helicopter view of the elements of the constellation of Joe Kincheloe's incredible critical project. In the foreground, within a bolder box, I have tried to highlight the issue or quest that was animating Joe at some moment in his incessant writing, and behind it I have captured, as best I could, one or two phrases or themes that struck me as emerging from Joe's worrying, interrogating and reworking of that particular issue (Figure 5.1).

There are several things that strike me in looking at the corpus of work of a truly remarkable critical scholar who really does encapsulate Paulo Freire's *Pedagogy of the Oppressed* in contemporary times, and it includes the following:

- A preparedness and a capacity to look deeply into all manner of cracks and crevices for topics that need to be revealed, exposed, unmasked and subjected to the bright glare of criticality in order to reconstruct them with a more democratic intent – this is what gives criticality its breadth, depth and reach as a coherent and authentic project.
- The courage to fearlessly tackle, in a systematic, scholarly and analytically rigorous way, the major shibboleths of neo-liberalism and capitalist culture, while exposing their complicit compradors – and refusing to be cowed or intimidated.
- A willingness to forthrightly name the issues that are deeply insinuated in and masquerade under the synthetic guise of 'reforms' – when in reality what they are doing is deforming, damaging, corrupting and corroding our democracies.
- To puncture the stupidity and nonsense that there is such a thing as disinterested, neutral, objectivist, value-free knowledge – and

145

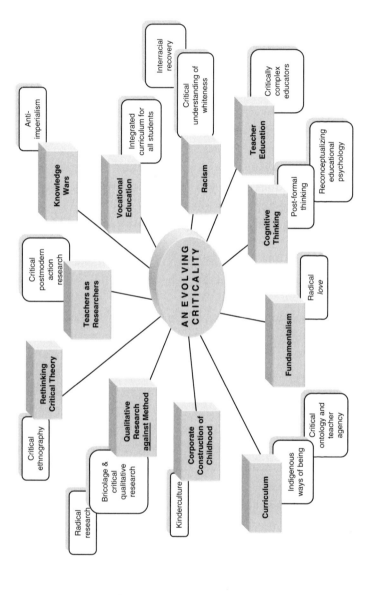

Figure 5.1 An Evolving Criticality.

contest the 'big lie' by demonstrating how theory is inextricably embedded in the practice and the experience of everyday lives, and how practice, experience and everyday lives are reshaped and reinformed by theory.

- To approach all of the above in ways that remain ethically grounded – which means understanding things from the vantage point of the 'least advantaged' – and honoring those perspectives both in the process of inquiry as well as in the forms in which those inquiries are conveyed and represented to others.
- Above all, to sustain the notion of 'co-generative dialogue' (Tobin, 2011, p. xx) by ensuring that everyone involved is brought into the conversation, thus extending the conversation in ways that expand the boundaries and identify the hopeful possibilities, enabling a confronting of obstacles and interferences.

I hope this book is a modest contribution to all of these worthy ideals.

References

Alinsky, S. (1989a). *Rules for Radicals: A Pragmatic Primer for Realistic Radicals.* New York, Vintage.
— (1989b, rev edn). *Reveille for Radicals.* New York, Vintage Books.
Anyon, J. (2005). *Radical Possibilities: Public Policy, Urban Education and a New Social Movement.* New York, Routledge.
Apple, M. (1971). 'The Hidden Curriculum and the Nature of Conflict.' *Interchange* 2(4): 27–40.
— (1975). 'Scientific Interests and the Nature of Educational Institutions.' In *Curriculum Theorizing: The Reconceptualists,* W. Pinar (ed.). Berkeley, McCutchan: 120–30.
— (1983). 'Work, Gender, and Teaching.' *Teachers College Record* 84(3): 611–28.
Apple, M., and K. Teitelbaum (1986). 'Are Teachers Losing Control of Their Skills and Curriculum?' *Journal of Curriculum Studies* 18(2): 177–84.
Aronowitz, S., and H. Giroux (1985). *Education Under Siege: The Conservative, Liberal and Radical Debate Over Schooling.* London, Routledge and Kegan Paul.
Australian Centre for Equity through Education and Australian Youth Research Centre (2001). 'Building Relationships: Making Education Work – A Report on the Perspectives of Young People.' Canberra, Commonwealth of Australia.
Avis, J. (2005). 'Beyond Performativity: Reflections on Activist Professionalism and the Labour Process in Further Education.' *Journal of Education Policy* 20(2): 209–22.
Ayers, W., J. Hunt and T. Quinn (1998). *Teaching for Social Justice: A Democracy and Education Reader.* New York, Teachers College Press.

Berlak, A. (1985). *Back to the Basics: Liberating Pedagogy and the Liberal Arts*. Paper presented at the Annual Meeting of the American Educational Research Association, Chicago, April.

Berliner, D., and B. Biddle (1995). *The Manufactured Crisis: Myths, Fraud, and the Attack on America's Public Schools*. Reading, MA, Addison-Wesley Publishing.

Bigelow, W. (1990). 'Inside the Classroom: Social Vision and Critical Pedagogy.' *Teachers College Record* **91**(3): 437–48.

— (1992). 'Inside the Classroom: Social Vision and Critical Pedagogy.' *Education Links* **2**(4): 351–7.

— (1998). 'The Human Lives Behind the Labels, the Global Sweatshop, Nike and the Race to the Bottom.' In *Teaching for Social Justice: A Democracy and Education Reader*, W. Ayers, J. Hunt and T. Quinn (eds). New York, Teachers College Press: 21–38.

Bingham, C., and A. Sidorkin (eds) (2004). *No Education Without Relation*. New York, Peter Lang Publishing.

Bourdieu, P. ([1986] 1997). 'Forms of Capital.' In *Education: Culture, Economy and Society*, A. Halsey, H. Lauder, P. Brown and A. Wells (eds). Oxford and New York, Oxford University Press: 46–58.

Boyte, H. (1980). *The Backyard Revolution: Understanding the New Citizen Movement*. Philadelphia, Temple University Press.

— (1989). *Commonwealth: A Return to Citizen Politics*. New York, Free Press.

Braverman, H. (1975). *Labor and Monopoly Capital: The Degradation of Work in the Twentieth Century*. New York, Monthly Review Press.

Brent, J. (2009). *Searching for Community: Representation, Power and Action on an Urban Estate*. Bristol, Policy Press.

Bridgeland, J., J. M. Dilulio and K. B. Morison (2006). *The Silent Epidemic: Perspectives of High School Dropouts*. Washington, DC, Civic Enterprises for the Bill and Melinda Gates Foundation.

Brown, L. (2003). *All My Relations: Community Building in Difficult Times*. British Columbia, Centre for Innovative Teaching, University of Victoria.

Bryk, A., and B. Schneider (2002). *Trust in Schools: A Core Resource for Improvement*. New York, Russell Sage Foundation.

Bryson, L., and M. Mowbray (1981). '"Community": The Spray-On Solution.' *Australian Journal of Social Issues* **16**(4): 255–66.

— (2005). 'More Spray-On Solution: Community Social Capital and Evidence Based Policy.' *Australian Journal of Social Issues* **40**(1): 91–106.

Carlson, D. (1987). 'Teachers as Political Actors.' *Harvard Educational Review* **57**(3): 283–306.

— (2005). 'Hope without Illusion: Telling the Story of Democratic Educational Renewal.' *International Journal of Qualitative Studies in Education* **18**(1): 21–45.

Carlson, D., and M. Apple (eds) (1998). *Power/Knowledge/Pedagogy.* Boulder, CO, Westview Press.

Carr, W., and S. Kemmis (1983). *Becoming Critical: Knowing Through Action Research.* Geelong, Victoria, Deakin University Press.

Carson, W. (2004). 'Is Communalism Dead? Reflections on the Present and Future of Crime Prevention.' *Australian and New Zealand Journal of Criminology* **37**(1): 1–21.

Cass, B., and D. Brennan (2002). 'Communities of Support or Communities of Surveillance and Enforcement in Welfare Reform Debates.' *Australian Journal of Social Issues* **37**(3): 247–62.

Chambers, E., and M. Cowan (2004). *Roots for Radicals: Organizing for Power, Action and Justice.* New York, Continuum.

Chapman, M., and K. Kirk (2001). *Lessons for Community Capacity Building: A Summary of the Research Evidence* A Research Review to Scottish Homes. School of Planning and Housing, Edinburgh College of Art, Heriot-Watt University, Edinburgh.

Cochran-Smith, M. (1991). 'Learning to Teach Against the Grain.' *Harvard Educational Review* **61**(3): 279–310.

Codd, J. (2005). 'Teachers as "Managed Professionals" in the Global Education Industry: The New Zealand Experience.' *Educational Review* **57**(2): 193–206.

Coleman, J. (1988). 'Social Capital in the Creation of Human Capital.' *American Journal of Sociology*, **94**(Supplement), S95–120.

Comer, J. (1993). *School Power: Implications for an Intervention Project.* New York, Free Press.

— (2004). *Leave No Child Behind: Preparing Today's Youth for Tomorrow's World*. New Haven, Yale University Press.

Connell, R. (1993). *Schools and Social Justice*. Toronto, Our Schools/Our Selves Education Foundation.

— (1994). 'Equity Through Education – Directions for Action.' Canberra, Australia, Address to Australian Centre for Equity through Education.

— (1996). *Prepare for Interesting Times: Education in a Fractured World* (Inaugural professorial address): University of Sydney, 6 August.

— (1998). 'Social Change and Curriculum Futures.' *Change: Transformations in Education* 1(1): 84–90.

Corbett, M. (2009a). 'Rural Schooling in Mobile Modernity: Returning to the Places I've Been.' *Journal of Research in Rural Education* 24(7): retrieved from http://jrre.psu.edu/articles/24_7.pdf on 26 January 2011.

— (2009b). 'Assimilation, Resistance, Rapprochement, and Loss: Response to Woodrum, Faircloth, Greenwood, and Kelly.' *Journal of Research in Rural Education* 24(12): retrieved from http://jrre.psu.edu/articles/24_12.pdf on 26 Jan 2011.

Cox, R. (1980). 'Social Forces, States and World Orders' Millenium.' *Millenium: Journal of International Studies* 10(2): 126–55.

Craig, G. (2003). 'Editorial Introduction.' *Community Development Journal* 38(1): 1–5.

— (2007). 'Community Capacity-Building: Something Old, Something New . . . ?' *Critical Social Policy* 27(3): 335–59.

de Certeau, M. (1984). *The Practice of Everyday Life*. Berkeley, University of California Press.

Dei, G., J. Mazzuca, E. McIsaac and J. Zin (1997). *Reconstructing 'Dropout': A Critical Ethnography of Black Students' Disengagement from School*. Toronto, University of Toronto Press.

Delgado, G. (1986). *Organizing the Movement: The Roots and Growth of ACORN*. Philadelphia, Temple University Press.

Department of Education and Early Childhood Development (2008). *Blueprint for Early Childhood Development and School Reform*.

Melbourne, Department of Education and Early Childhood Development.

Duncan-Andrade, J. (2009). 'Note to Educators: Hope Required When Growing Roses in Concrete.' *Harvard Educational Review* 19(2): 181–94.

Eade, D. (1997). *Capacity-Building: An Approach to People-Centered Development.* Oxford, Oxfam.

Erickson, F. (1982). 'Classroom Discourse as Improvisation: Relationship between Academic Task Structure and Social Participation Structures in Lessons.' In *Communicating in the Classroom*, L. Wilkinson (ed.). New York, Academic Press: 153–81.

— (1987). 'Transformation and School Success: The Politics and Culture of School Achievement.' *Anthropology and Education Quarterly* 18(4): 335–56.

Everingham, C. (2003). *Social Justice and the Politics of Community.* Aldershot, Ashgate.

Fagan, G. (1995). *Culture, Politics, and Irish School Dropouts: Constructing Political Identities.* Westport, CT, Bergin & Garvey.

Feiman-Nemser, S., and R. Floden (1986). 'The Cultures of Teaching.' In *Third Handbook of Research on Teaching*, M. Wittrock (ed.). New York, Collier-Macmillan: 505–26.

Fielding, M. (1999) Setting, Policy Pathology and Student Perspectives: Learning to Labour in New Times.' *Cambridge Journal of Education* 29(2): 277–87.

Fielding, M. (2001). 'Target Setting, Policy Pathology and Student Perspectives: Learning to Labour in New Times.' In *Taking Education Really Seriously: Four Years' Hard Labour*, M. Fielding (ed.). London and New York, RoutledgeFalmer: 143–54.

Fine, M. (1991). *Framing Dropouts: Notes on the Politics of an Urban Public High School.* Albany, State University of New York Press.

Fraser, J., P. Davis, and R. Singh (1997). 'Identity Work by Alternative High School Students.' *International Journal of Qualitative Studies in Education* 10(2): 221–35.

Freebody, P., C. Ludwig, and S. Gunn (1995). *Everyday Literacy Practices In and Out of Schools in Low Socio-Economic Urban Communities*. Melbourne, Curriculum Corporation.

Freire, P. (1972a). *Pedagogy of the Oppressed*. Harmondsworth, Penguin.

— (1972b). *Cultural Action for Freedom*. Harmondsworth, Penguin.

— (1996). *Pedagogy of Hope: Reliving Pedagogy of the Oppressed*. New York, Continuum.

— (1998). *Pedagogy of Freedom: Ethics, Democracy, and Civic Courage*. Lanham, MD, Rowman & Littlefield.

— (2004). *Pedagogy of Indignation*. Boulder, CO, Paradigm Press.

— (2007). *Daring to Dream: Toward a Pedagogy of the Unfinished*. Boulder, CO, Paradigm Publishers.

Fried, R. (1980). *Empowerment V's Delivery of Services*. Concord, NH, New Hampshire State Department of Education.

Garrison, D. (1991). 'Critical Thinking and Adult Education: A Conceptual Model for Developing Critical Thinking in Adult Learners.' *International Journal of Lifelong Education* 10(4): 287–303.

Gecan, M. (2004). *Going Public: An Organizer's Guide to Citizen Action*. New York, Anchor Books.

Giddens, A. (1979). *Central Problems of Social Theory: Action, Structure and Contradiction in Social Analysis*. London, Macmillan.

Gilligan, C. (1982). *In a Different Voice*. Cambridge, MA, Harvard University Press.

Gilroy, P. (1993). *The Black Atlantic: Modernity and Double Consciousness*. Cambridge, MA, Harvard University Press.

Ginsburg, M. (1988). 'Educators as Workers and Political Actors in Britain and North America.' *British Journal of Sociology of Education* 9(3): 359–67.

Giroux, H. (1979). 'Schooling and the Culture of Positivism: Notes on the Death of History.' *Educational Theory* 29(4): 263–84.

— (1981). 'Pedagogy, Pessimism and the Politics of Conformity: A Reply to Linda McNeil.' *Curriculum Inquiry* 11(3): 211–22.

— (1983). *Theory and Resistance in Education: A Pedagogy for the Opposition*. South Hadley, MA, Bergin & Garvey.

— (1985a). 'Intellectual Labour and Pedagogical Work: Re-Thinking the Role of the Teacher as Intellectual.' *Phenomenology and Pedagogy* **3**(1): 20–32.

— (1985b). 'Critical Pedagogy and the Resisting Intellectual.' *Phenomenology and Pedagogy* **3**(2): 84–97.

— (1985c). 'Teachers as Transformative Intellectuals.' *Social Education* **49**(May): 376–9.

— (1988). *Teachers as Intellectuals: Toward a Critical Pedagogy of Learning.* Granby, MA, Bergin and Garvey.

Giroux, H., and P. McLaren (1986). 'Teacher Education and the Politics of Engagement: The Case for Democratic Schooling.' *Harvard Educational Review* **56**(3): 213–38.

Giroux, H., and M. Schmidt (2004). 'Closing the Achievement Gap: A Metaphor for Children Left Behind.' *Journal of Educational Change* **5**: 213–28.

Gittell, R., and A. Vidal (1998). *Community Organizing: Building Social Capital as a Development Strategy.* Thousand Oaks, CA, Sage Publications.

Glazier, J. (2005). 'Talking and Teaching through a Positional Lens: Recognizing What and Who We Privilege in Our Practice.' *Teaching Education* **16**(3): 231–43.

Gold, E., E. Simon, and C. Brown (2005). 'A New Conception of Parent Engagement: Community Organizing for School Reform.' In *Sage Handbook of Educational Leadership: Advances in Theory, Research and Practice,* F. English (ed.). Thousand Oaks, CA, Sage Publishing: 237–68.

Gold, E., and E. Simon with C. Brown (2002). *Successful Community Organizing for School Reform. Strong Neighbourhoods Strong Schools. The Indicators Project on Education Organizing.* Chicago, IL, Cross City Campaign for Urban School Reform.

Goodman, J. (1992). *Elementary Schooling for Critical Democracy.* Albany, NY, State University of New York Press.

Grace, G. (1994). 'Urban Education and the Culture of Contentment: The Politics, Culture, and Economics of Inner-City Schooling.' In *Education in Urban Areas: Cross-National Dimensions,* N. Stromquist (ed.). Westport, CT, Praeger: 45–59.

Gramsci, A. (1971). *Selection from the Prison Notebooks*. New York, International Publishers.

Greene, M. (1985). *Teacher as Project: Choice, Perspective, and the Public Space*. Summer Institute of Teaching, New York, Columbia University.

Gunter, H. (2006). 'Confounding Stereotypes: Risk, Resilience and Achievement in Urban Schools.' In *Improving Urban Schools: Leadership and Collaboration*, M. Ainscow and M. West (eds). Maidenhead, UK, Open University Press: 58–69.

Haberman, M. (1991). 'The Pedagogy of Poverty Versus Good Teaching.' *Phi Delta Kappan* 73(4): 290–4.

Hatton, E. (1988). 'Teachers' Work as Bricolage: Implications for Teacher Education.' *British Journal of Sociology of Education* 9(3): 337–57.

— (1997). 'Teacher Educators and the Production of Bricoleurs: An Ethnographic Study.' *International Journal of Qualitative Studies in Education* 10(2): 237–57.

hayes, k., S. Steinberg, and K. Tobin (eds) (2011). *Key Works in Critical Pedagogy: Joe L. Kincheloe*. Rotterdam, The Netherlands: Sense Publishers.

Honan, E. (2004). 'Teachers as Bricoleurs: Producing Plausible Readings or Curriculum Documents.' *English Teaching: Practice and Critique* 3(2): 99–112.

— (2006). Teachers as Bricoleurs Resisting Mandated Curriculum. In *Discourse, Resistance and Identity Formation*, J. Sattherwaite, W. Martin and L. Roberts (eds). Stoke-on-Trent, Trentham Books: 79–95.

hooks, b. (1990). *Yearning: Race, Gender and Cultural Politics*. Boston, South End Press.

Horwitt, S. (1989). *Let Them Call Me a Rebel: Saul Alinsky, His Life and Legacy*. New York, Knopf.

Huberman, M. (1983). 'Recipes for Busy Kitchens.' *Knowledge, Creation, Diffusion, Utilization* 4(4): 478–510.

— (1988). *Teacher Professionalism and Workplace Conditions*. The Holmes Group conference on Conceptions of Teachers' Work, East Lansing, Michigan State University.

— (1990). *The Social Context of Instruction in Schools*. Paper Presented at the Annual Meeting of American Education Research Association, Boston, MA, April.

Illich, I. (1971). *Deschooling Society*. New York, Harper Colophon Books.

Johnson, R. (2009). 'Introduction. No Easy Answers: Jeremy Brent, Southmead and "Community".' In *Searching for Community: Representation, Power and Action on an Urban Estate*, J. Brent (ed.). Bristol, Policy Press: 1–10.

Keith, N. (1999). 'Whose Community Schools? New Discourses, Old Patterns.' *Theory into Practice* 38(4): 225–34.

Kohl, H. (1983). 'Examining Closely What We Do.' *Learning* 12(1): 28–30.

— (1994). *'I Won't Learn From You' and Other Thoughts on Creative Maladjustment*. New York, The New Press.

Kreisberg, S. (1992). *Transforming Power: Domination, Empowerment and Education*. Albany, State University of New York Press.

Lather, P. (1986). 'Research as praxis.' *Harvard Educational Review* 56(3), 257–77.

Levinson, B. (1992). 'Ogbu's Anthropology and Critical Ethnography of Education: A Reciprocal Interrogation.' *International Journal of Qualitative Studies in Education* 5(3): 205–25.

Makuwira, J. (2007a). 'The Politics of Community Capacity-Building: Contestations, Contradictions, Tensions and Ambivalences in the Discourse in Indigenous Communities in Australia.' *Australian Journal of Indigenous Education* 36(Suppl.): 129–36.

— (2007b). 'Community Organizing.' In *Encyclopedia of Activism and Social Justice, Volumes 1, 2 & 3*, G. Anderson and K. Herr (eds). Thousand Oaks, CA, Sage Publications: 383–5.

Marmot, M. (2007). 'Achieving Health Equity: From Root Causes to Fair Outcomes.' *Lancet* 370: 1153–63.

— (2010). *Fair Society, Healthy Lives: Strategic Review of Health Inequalities in England Post 2010*. London, The Marmot Review.

May, S. (1994). *Making Multicultural Education Work*. Clevedon, Multilingual Matters.

McDonald, C., and G. Marston (2002). 'Fixing the Niche? Rhetorics of the Community Sector in the Neo-Liberal Welfare Regime.' *Just Policy* 27(August): 3–10.

McLaren, P. (1986). *Schooling as Ritual Performance*. Boston, Routledge and Kegan Paul.

McPeck, J. (1981). *Critical Thinking and Education*. New York, St. Martin's Press.

Mediratta, K. (2004 September). *Constituents of Change: Community Organizations and Public Education Reform*. New York, New York University, Institute for Education and Social Policy.

Mediratta, K., and Fruchter, N. (2001). *Mapping the Field or Organizing for School Improvement: A Report on Education Organizing*. New York, Institute for Education and Social Policy, New York University.

Mediratta, K., N. Fruchter, and A. Lewis (2002). *Organizing for School Reform: How Communities are Finding their Voices and reclaiming their Public Schools. A Report*. New York: New York University, Institute for Education and Social Policy.

Mediratta, K., and J. Karp (2003). *Parent Power and Urban School Reform: The Story of Mothers on the Move*. New York, Institute for Education and Social Policy, New York University.

Mediratta, K., S. Shaha, S. McAlister, N. Fruchter, C. Mokhtar, and D. Lockwood (2008). *Organized Communities, Stronger Schools. A Preview of Research Findings*. Providence, RI: Annenburg Institue for School Reform at Brown University.

Meier, D. (1995). *The Power of Their Ideas: Lessons for America from a Small School in Harlem*. Boston, Beacon.

Mitchell, C., and L. Sackney (2001). 'Building Capacity for a Learning Community.' *Canadian Journal of Educational Administration and Policy* 19(24 February): 1–3.

Mowbray, M. (2004). 'Beyond Community Capacity Building: The Effect of Government on Social Capital.' Retrieved from http://www.obs-pascal.com/resources/mowbray2004.pdf on 21 May 2008.

— (2005). 'Community Capacity Building or State Opportunism?' *Community Development Journal* 40(3): 255–64.

Nader, C. (2008). 'In Search of a Way to Involve All.' *The Age*. Melbourne, 24 May: 6.

Nash, V., and I. Christie (2003). *Making Sense of Community*. London, Institute for Public Policy Research.

National Governors Association (28 February 2007). 'National Summit on America's "Silent Epidemic" to Highlight America's Response to the Dropout Crisis.' *News Release*.

Newmann, F. (ed.) (1992). *Student Engagement and Achievement in American Secondary Schools*. New York, Teachers College Press.

Newmann, F., and Associates (eds) (1996). *Authentic Achievement: Restructuring Schools for Intellectual Quality*. San Francisco, CA, Jossey-Bass Publishers.

Newmann, F., and G. Wehlage (1995). *Successful School Restructuring: A Report to the Public by the Center on Organization and Restructuring of Schools*. Madison, WI, Center on Organization and Restructuring of Schools, University of Wisconsin-Madison.

Noblit, G. (1993). 'Power and Caring.' *American Educational Research Journal* **30**(1): 23–38.

Noddings, N. (2005). 'What Does It Mean to Educate the Whole Child?' *Educational Leadership* **63**(1): 8–13.

Northern Territory Government (2004). *Report on Future Directions for Secondary Education in the Northern Territory*. Darwin, Charles Darwin University; Northern Territory Government, Department of Employment Education and Training.

Oakes, J., J. Rogers and M. Lipton (2006). *Learning Power: Organizing for Education and Justice*. New York, Teachers College Press.

Ogbu, J. (1982). 'Cultural Discontinuities and Schooling.' *Anthropology and Education Quarterly* **13**(4): 290–307.

O'Loughlin, M. (1994). 'Daring the Imagination: Unlocking Voices of Dissent and Possibility in Teaching.' *Theory into Practice* **34**(2): 107–16.

Orfield, G. (ed.) (2004). *Dropouts in America: Confronting the Graduation Rate Crisis*. Cambridge: MA, Harvard Education Press.

Orr, M. (ed.) (2007). *Transforming the City: Community Organizing and the Challenge of Political Change.* Lawrence, University Press of Kansas.

Osterman, P. (2002). *Gathering Power: The Future of Progressive Politics in America.* Boston, Beacon Press.

Perlstein, D. (2005). *Justice, Justice: School Politics and the Eclipse of Liberalism.* New York, Peter Lang.

Pollard, A., P. Broadfoot, A. Osborne, and D. Abbot (1994). *Changing English Primary Schools: the Impact of the Education Reform Act at Key Stage One.* London, Cassell.

Popkewitz, T. (1987). *Critical Studies in Teacher Education: Its Folklore, Theory and Practice.* London and Philadelphia, Falmer Press.

Poplin, M., and Weeres, J. (eds). (1992). *Voices from the Inside: Report on Schooling Inside the Classroom: Executive Summary.* Claremont, CA, Claremont Graduate School.

Postman, N., and C. Weingartner (1971). *The Soft Revolution: A Student Handbook for Turning Schools Around.* New York, Delacorte Press.

Pratt, L. (1991). 'Arts of the Contact Zone.' *Profession* **91**: 33–40.

Productivity Commission. (2003). 'Report on Government Services 2003.' Retrieved from http://www.pc.gov.au/gsp/2003/index.html on 1 February 2003.

Putnam, R. (2000). *Bowling Alone: The Collapse and Revival of American Community.* New York, Simon & Schuster.

Raider-Roth, M. (2005a). *Trusting What You Know: The High Stakes of Classroom Relationships.* San Francisco, Jossey Bass.

— (2005b). 'Trusting What You Know: Negotiating the Relational Context of Classroom Life.' *Teachers College Record* **107**(4): 587–628.

Razack, S. (1993). 'Teaching Activists for Social Change: Coming to Grips with Questions of Subjectivity and Domination.' *Canadian Journal for the Study of Adult Education* **7**(2): 65–78.

Roberts, P. (1997). 'Paulo Freire and Political Correctness.' *Educational Philosophy and Theory* **29**: 81–101.

Romano, R. (2000). *Forging an Educative Community: The Wisdom of Love, the Power of Understanding, and the Terror of It All.* New York, Peter Lang.

Romano, R., and G. Glascock (2002). *Hungry Minds in Hard Times: Educating for Complexity for Students of Poverty.* New York, Peter Lang Publishing.

Ryan, B. (1982). 'Accountability in Australian Education.' *Discourse* 2(2): 21–40.

Sachs, J. (2000). 'The Activist Professional.' *Journal of Educational Change* 1(1): 7–95.

— (2002). *The Activist Teaching Profession.* Buckingham, Open University Press.

Saegert, S., J. Thompson and M. Warren (eds) (2001). *Social Capital and Poor Communities.* New York, Russell Sage Foundation.

Sanders, M. (1970). *The Professional Radical: Conversations with Saul Alinsky.* New York, Harper and Row.

Sawyer, R. (2001). *Creating Conversations: Improvisation in Everyday Discourse.* Cresskill, NJ, Hampton Press.

— (2004). 'Improvised Lessons: Collaborative Discussions in the Contructivist Classroom.' *Teaching Education* 15(2): 189–201.

Shirley, D. (1997). *Community Organizing for Urban School Reform.* Austin, University of Texas Press.

— (2002). *Valley Interfaith and School Reform.* Austin, University of Texas Press.

Shor, I. (1980). *Critical Teaching and Everyday Life.* Chicago, University of Chicago Press.

— (1996). *When Students Have Power: Negotiating Authority in a Critical Pedagogy.* Chicago and London, University of Chicago Press.

Shor, I., and P. Freire (1987). *Pedagogy for Liberation: Dialogues on Transforming Education.* Westport, CT, Bergin and Garvey.

Sidorkin, A. (2002). *Learning Relations.* New York, Peter Lang.

Simon, R. (1984). 'Signposts for a Critical Pedagogy: A Review of Henry Giroux's Theory and Resistance in Education.' *Educational Theory* 34(4): 379–88.

— (1985). 'Critical Pedagogy.' In *International Encyclopedia of Education Research and Studies*, T. Husen and T. Posthelwaite (eds). London, Pergamon Press. 2: 1118–20.

— (1992). *Teaching Against the Grain: Texts for a Pedagogy of Possibility*. Amherst, Bergin & Garvey.

Smith, A. (2007). 'Review of "Radical Possibilities: Public Policy, Urban Education, and a New Social Movement".' *Journal of Education Policy* **22**(6): 709–20.

Smith, N., L. Littlejohns and D. Thompson (2001). 'Cobwebs: Insights into Community Capacity and Its Relation to Health Outcomes.' *Community Development Journal* **36**(1): 30–41.

Smyth, J. (1984). 'Toward a "Critical Consciousness" in the Instructional Supervision of Experienced Teachers.' *Curriculum Inquiry* **14**(4): 425–36.

— (1985). 'Developing a Critical Practice of Clinical Supervision.' *Journal of Curriculum Studies* **17**(1): 1–15.

— (1986). 'Changing What We Do in Our Teaching: Let's Stop Talking about It!' *Journal of Teaching Practice* **6**(2): 16–31.

— (1987). *Rationale for Teachers' Critical Pedagogy: A Handbook.* Geelong,Victoria, Deakin University Press.

— (1991). *Teachers as Collaborative Learners: Challenging Dominant Forms of Supervision.* London, Open University Press.

— (1993). 'A Socially Critical Approach to Teacher Education.' In *Teacher Educators: Annual Handbook 1993*, T. Simpson (ed.). Brisbane, Queensland University of Technology: 153–65.

— (1995a). 'Teachers' Work and the Labour Process of Teaching: Central Problematics in Professional Development.' In *Professional Development in Education: New Paradigms and Practices*, T. Guskey and M. Huberman (eds). New York, Teachers College Press: 69–91.

— (1995b). *Some Possible Candidates for Classroom Observation by Socially Critical Teachers and Colleagues.* Adelaide, Flinders Institute for the Study of Teaching.

— (1998, December). *Dialectical Theory-Building: Juxtaposing Theory with Student Voices in the Non-Completion of Schooling.* Paper presented at the annual meeting of the Australian Association for Research in Education, Adelaide.

— (2004). 'Social Capital and the "Socially Just School".' *British Journal of Sociology of Education* **25**(1): 19–33.

— (2005a). 'Modernizing the Australian Education Workplace: A Case of Failure to Deliver for Teachers of Young Disadvantaged Adolescents.' *Educational Review* **57**(2): 221–33.

— (2005b). 'An Argument for New Understandings and Explanations of Early School Leaving That Go beyond the Conventional.' *London Review of Education* **3**(2): 117–30.

— (2006a). 'When Students Have "Relational Power": The School as a Site for Identity Formation around Engagement and School Retention.' Paper presented at the annual meeting of the Australian Association for Research in Education. Adelaide.

— (2006b). 'Schools and Communities Put at a Disadvantage: Relational Power, Resistance, Boundary Work and Capacity Building in Educational Identity Formation.' *Journal of Learning Communities: International Journal of Learning in Social Contexts* **3**: 7–39.

— (2007). 'Teacher Development Against the Policy Reform Grain: An Argument for Recapturing Relationships in Teaching and Learning.' *Teacher Development: An International Journal of Teachers' Professional Development* **11**(2): 221–36.

— (2008). 'Beyond a Heroic View of Educational Leadership: A Critical Theory of Educational Leadership That Builds on the Legacy of Saul Alinsky's View of Community Organizing.' Presentation to Critical Leadership Studies class, University of Manchester, 12 March.

Smyth, J., L. Angus, B. Down, and P. McInerney (2009). *Activist and Socially Critical School and Community Renewal: Social Justice in Exploitative Times.* Rotterdam, The Netherlands, Sense Publishers.

Smyth, J., B. Down, and P. McInerney (2010). *'Hanging in With Kids' in Tough Times: Engagement in Contexts of Educational Disadvantage in the Relational School.* New York: Peter Lang Publishing.

Smyth, J., R. Hattam, J. Cannon, J. Edwards, N. Wilson, and S. Wurst (2000). *Listen to Me, I'm Leaving: Early School Leaving in South Australian Secondary Schools.* Adelaide, Flinders Institute for the Study of Teaching; Department of Employment, Education and Training; and Senior Secondary Assessment Board of South Australia.

Smyth, J., R. Hattam, and M. Lawson (eds) (1998). *Schooling for a Fair Go*. Sydney, Federation Press.

Smyth, J., Hattam, R., with Cannon, J., Edwards, J., Wilson, N., & Wurst, S. (2004). *'Dropping Out', Drifting Off, Being Excluded: Becoming Somebody Without School*. New York, Peter Lang Publishing.

Smyth, J., and P. McInerney (2007a). *Teachers in the Middle: Reclaiming the Wasteland of the Adolescent Years of Schooling*. New York, Peter Lang Publishing.

— (2007b). "'Living on the Edge": A Case of School Reform Working for Disadvantaged Adolescents.' *Teachers College Record* 109(5): 1123–70.

Smyth, J., P. McInerney and S. Harrison (2011). *What to Look for in Genuine Community Engagement: A Toolkit*. Ballarat, Victoria, University of Ballarat.

Smyth, J., P. McInerney, and R. Hattam (2003). 'Tackling School Leaving at Its Source: A Case of Reform in the Middle Years of Schooling.' *British Journal of Sociology of Education* 24(2): 177–93.

Smyth, J., and G. Shacklock (1998). *Re-Making Teaching: Ideology, Policy and Practice*. London and New York, Routledge.

Snow, D., and L. Anderson (1987). 'Identity Work Among the Homeless: The Verbal Construction and Avowal of Personal Identities.' *American Journal of Sociology* 92(6): 1336–71.

Snyder, C. (2002). 'Hope Theory: Rainbows in the Mind.' *Psychological Review* 13(4): 249–75.

Solomon, D. (2005). Questions for Jonathan Kozol: School Monitor. *New York Times Magazine*. New York: 14.

Stanton-Salazar, R. (2001). *Manufacturing Hope and Despair: The School and Kin Support Networks of U.S. Mexican Youth*. New York, Teachers College Press.

State Government of Victoria (2005a). *Challenges in Addressing Disadvantage in Victoria: Reporting on Progress Identifying Future Directions*. Melbourne, Department of Premier and Cabinet.

State Government of Victoria (2005b). *A Fairer Victoria: Creating Opportunities and Addressing Disadvantage*. Melbourne, Department of Premier and Cabinet.

— (2006a). *A Fairer Victoria: Case Studies*. Melbourne, Department of Premier and Cabinet, Victorian Government.

— (2006b). *A Fairer Victoria: Progress and Next Steps*. Melbourne, State Government of Victoria.

Stone, C., K. Doherty, C. Jones, and T. Ross (1999). 'Schools in Disadvantaged Neighborhoods: The Community Development Challenge.' In *Urban Problems and Community Development*, R. Ferguson and W. Dickens (eds). Washington, DC, Brookings Institution Press: 339–80.

Syme, S. (2004). 'Social Determinants of Health: The Community as Empowered Partner.' *Preventing Chronic Disease: Public Health Research, Practice and Policy* 1(1): 1–4.

Thomson, P. (2005). 'Who's Afraid of Saul Alinsky? Radical Traditions in Community Organizing.' *Forum* 47(1 & 2): 199–206.

Tobin, J. (2011). 'Learning from a Good Mate: An Introduction.' In *Key Works in Critical Pedagogy: Joe L. Kincheloe*, k. hayes, S. Steinberg, and K. Tobin (eds). Rotterdam, The Netherlands: Sense Publishers: xv–xxiv.

US Department of Education (1986). *What Works: Research about Teaching and Learning*. Washington, DC,US Department of Education.

Valenzuela, A. (1999). *Subtractive Schooling: U.S.-Mexican Youth and the Politics of Caring*. New York, State University of New York Press.

Van Manen, M. (1977). 'Linking Ways of Knowing with Ways of Being Practical.' *Curriculum Inquiry* 6: 205–28.

Verity, F. (2007). 'Community Capacity Building – A Review of the Literature.' Adelaide, School of Social Administration and Social Work, Flinders University of South Australia. Report for the Department of Health, Health Promotion Branch, Government of South Australia.

Vibert, A., J. Portelli, and V. Leighteizer (2001). *Student Engagement in Learning and School Life: Case Reports from Project Schools, Volume 1 Part III: Nova Scotia*. Montreal, Ed-Lex, Faculty of Law, McGill University.

REFERENCES

Vibert, A., J. Portelli, V. Leighteizer, with Forrest, M., and B. Will (2001). *Student Engagement in Learning and School Life: Case Reports from Project Schools, Volume 1 Part III: Nova Scotia.* Montreal, Ed-Lex, Faculty of Law, McGill University.

Vibert, A., J. Portelli, C. M. Shields, and L. LaRocque (2002). 'Critical Practice in Elementary Schools: Voice, Community, and a Curriculum for Life.' *Journal of Educational Change* 3(2): 93–116.

Warham, S. (1993). 'Reflection on Hegemony: Towards a Model of Teacher Competence.' *Educational studies* 19(2): 205–17.

Warren, M. (2001). *Dry Bones Rattling: Community Building to Revitalize American Democracy.* Princeton, Princeton University Press.

— (2004). 'Linking Community Development and School Improvement.' A report prepared for the Ford Foundation. Retrieved from http://www.lsna.net/display.aspx?pointer=2515 on 3 June 2008.

— (2005). 'Communities and Schools: A New View of Urban School Reform.' *Harvard Educational Review* 75(2): 133–73.

— (2007). 'Linking Community Development and School Improvement. An Interview with Professor Mark Warren.' *Community Investments* **Fall**: 16–18.

Warren, M., and R. Wood (2001). *Faith-based community Organizing: The State of the Field.* Jericho, NY, Interfaith Funders.

Webb, D. (2010). 'Paulo Freire and "The Need for a Kind of Education in Hope".' *Cambridge Journal of Education* 40(4): 327–39.

Wilkinson, R. (2005). *The Impact of Inequality: How to Make Sick Societies Healthier.* New York, The New Press.

Wilkinson, R., and M. Marmot (eds) (2003). *Social Determinants of Health: Solid Facts*, 2nd edn. Copenhagen, Denmark, WHO Regional Office for Europe.

Wilkinson, R., and K. Pickett (2009). *The Spirit Level: Why More Equal Societies Almost Always Do Better.* London, Allen Lane.

Williams, M. (1989). *Neighborhood Organizing for Urban School Reform.* New York, Teachers College Press.

Willie, C. (2000). 'Confidence, Trust and Respect: The Pre-Eminent Goals of Educational Reform.' *Journal of Negro Education* **69**(4): 255–63.

Willis, P. (1977). *Learning to Labor: How Working Class Kids Get Working Class Jobs.* Westmead, England, Gower.

Wood, G. (1988). 'Democracy and the Curriculum.' In *The Curriculum: Problems, Politics and Possibilities.* L. Beyer and M. Apple. Albany, NY, State University of New York Press: 166–90.

— (1990). 'Teachers as Curriculum Workers.' In *Teaching and Thinking About Curriculum*, J. Sears and D. Marshall (eds). New York, Teachers College Press: 97–110.

Wood, R. (2002). *Faith in Action: Religion, Race and Democratic Organizing in America.* Chicago, University of Chicago Press.

Zachary, E., and s. olatoye (2001). *A Case Study: Community Organizing for School Improvement in the South Bronx.* New York, Institute for Education and Social Policy, New York University.

Zeichner, K. (1983). 'Alternative Paradigms in Teacher Education.' *Journal of Teacher Education* **34**(3): 3–9.

— (1992). *Connecting Genuine Teacher Development to the Struggle for Social Justice.* East Lansing, National Center for Research on Teacher Learning, Michigan State University.

Author Index

Subject Index